Patrick Forsyth

The Teach Yourself series has been trusted around the world for over sixty years. This new series of 'In a Week' business books is designed to help people at all levels and around the world to further their careers. Learn in a week, what the experts learn in a lifetime.

Patrick Forsyth runs Touchstone Training & Consultancy and has worked, widely and internationally, as a trainer specializing in marketing and communications skills. He writes extensively on business matters and is the author of many successful books for managers and executives, all designed to offer proven, practical guidance on the skills required for job and career success.

Outstanding confidence

Patrick Forsyth

www.inaweek.co.uk

Teach Yourself®

Contents

Introduction

It is an old saying, and perhaps a sobering thought, that 'if you think you can, you can, and if you think you can't, you're right'. What often makes the difference between doing something successfully and failure is the level of confidence you bring to the task. The trick is to ensure you have sufficient confidence to bring.

Fear, uncertainty and a lack of (sufficient) confidence is a position all too easy to find yourself in. There always seem to be a hundred and one good reasons why something will be difficult, impossible or a disaster. Psychologists say that a huge amount of what they call 'self-talk' is instinctively negative. Faced with a task we naturally think first of the difficulties and too often go on to conclude that we will fail and/or not enjoy the process of trying. All our inner dialogue begins with something like 'I can't'.

Be assured that you are not unusual if you feel like this; you are normal.

I have a new book to write; this one. Okay, I have written others (including another in this series *Successful pitching for business in a week*), but it still remains a challenge. It's quite a job, it is a great many words, it's going to take some time and I am really not at all sure that I can ... oh dear; it really is all too easy to follow this path.

But actually, in reality, I am confident I can do this, do it well and complete it on time. But because I am thinking about this book and therefore about confidence, when I think about my situation I quickly realize that if I *am* confident it is because I have set out to be so. In other words, the good news at this stage is that you *can* be confident about things you do, even difficult ones. Realistically there are exceptions. I will doubtless never be able to juggle with flaming torches without burning holes in the carpet; indeed rashly believing I could do so would probably make a conflagration more likely, and no amount of confidence would make a difference (at least without extensive training and practice).

There is an important first lesson here.

Abraham Lincoln said something to the effect that a man obtains the level of happiness he *decides* to obtain. He was implicitly saying that you have to work at it. And obtaining a level of confidence, a useful level that actually acts to help you achieve something, while lessening the fears and discomfort about it, is very much the same. If you feel you currently lack confidence, in general or about some specific task, making a presentation, say, something that can understandably cause apprehension, then, be assured, it is possible to boost it.

A choice

You have a choice. Either you opt out: operating on whatever level of self-confidence circumstances bestow upon you, recognizing that human nature, the competitive workplace and other influences tend to exert a negative pressure to reduce the level of self-confidence you have. Or you adopt an active approach and determine that you will work at achieving a useful level of self-confidence despite all the world may throw at you. It really is a no-brainer, especially as much that you need to do to take control is straightforward.

View it the right way and take action to make it possible and confidence, and confidence in the workplace particularly (the focus here), *can* be increased. This book is designed to help. It sets out *practical* approaches, ways of thinking and ways of doing that will help you and it shows how very manageable some of those techniques are to deploy.

Perhaps the first thing to do is to make a simple, but firm, resolution to take control, to work actively to increase your overall self-confidence and that which affects specific tasks you want or must undertake. Heightened confidence can allow you not only to do more and do it better, it can change and improve your profile, making you seem more competent and professional in a way that, in an increasingly competitive workplace, can positively affect both your job and career.

Okay? Resolution made, let's see how you can put that resolution into effect. If you want to, or indeed need to, boost your confidence then I am confident the next seven chapters will help you do just that. Think positive, turn over and read on.

Patrick Forsyth

What is confidence?

The dictionary says confidence is 'a feeling of reliance or certainty, a sense of self-reliance; boldness'. We all understand this as the feeling that we can do something. This is not necessarily linked to perfection. With, say, a presentation to make you may know you are not the best orator in the world, but know also that you can do a good, workmanlike job of it that more than meets the needs of the occasion. Confidence is not just a feeling; it is something that actively works to help you do things. It may not negate the need for study, preparation or whatever but it boosts the likelihood of success in a tangible way. Furthermore, feeling confident can act to make you appear confident – professional, expert, or whatever is appropriate – and that too can help the process, in the way that an audience may sometimes already be thinking your presentation will be good even before you open your mouth.

Some people despair, believing that you are either born confident or not. Certainly people may have a natural tendency to feel confident, part inherent, part from background – the nurture aspect of their upbringing. But, without a doubt, natural tendency is only one factor, and in any case the most important message of this book is that your level of confidence is *not* fixed. Think about it. There is almost certainly something you can think of that you originally approached with little or no confidence and which you now view more positively having done it, perhaps repeatedly, and survived.

Of course, there may be things we never learn to love, but which, despite that, we are able to undertake with some equanimity, perhaps after experiment, review, training or practice; or all these things. But usually, whatever we fear doing, we can actually do with less fear if we decide to change our feelings and work at doing so.

Now we need to keep a clear perspective on confidence as we proceed here. It is not a panacea. No amount of confidence will make up for a level of information or skill that simply prohibits you from doing something. But the fact is there are things that you may be perfectly well able to do and yet a lack of confidence reduces your level of performance or, at worst, makes you fail. Furthermore a lack of confidence can have you avoiding things, things that should not be avoided, and risk you being judged harshly for doing so. Presenting, mentioned above, makes a good example as there is certainly a level of trauma involved and because of that many people lack confidence in standing up to speak in public. They avoid ever having to get into a position where they must do so. Yet such a task is so important in many jobs, and avoiding such things may be dangerous. I can well remember the Managing Director of a company where I was to conduct a training workshop on making presentations, starting his introduction by reminding people that 'no one gets promoted here unless they can make a good presentation'. True enough, yet not, with hindsight, a phrase to boost participants' confidence.

Consider an example, something I observed at a conference, and which demonstrates the very powerful effect confidence can have on events. One speaker amongst several, sitting in a

SUNDAY

MONDAY

TUESDAY

WEDNESDAY

THURSDAY

FRIDAY

SATURDAY

line on the platform next to the Chairman was introduced and rose to speak. He began seemingly in a routine manner: *Ladies and Gentlemen*, he said, *I know time is short, but in the hour I have available I will ....* The Chairman, who sat beside him, looked horrified, tugged his sleeve and pointed to his watch. The speaker glanced in his direction for a second, looked up and continued: *Of course, I am so sorry, in the half hour I am allocated...* As he said this he paused, lifted his notes, in the form of A4 sheets, and tore them in half lengthways down the page, throwing half of them behind him and thus apparently halving the duration of his talk. As the papers fluttered down he then continued – with every member of the group giving him their complete attention. The feeling amongst every one of the two hundred or so people in the room said, *This should be good.*

What he did had nothing whatsoever to do with his topic. It was a device, what I call a flourish, designed only to indicate that he was confident. It was probably planned with the Chairman, but that did not matter, the effect was palpable and it helped him make a good start. He clearly understood that confidence breeds confidence. He knew if he displayed confidence, then the audience would feel more confidence in what was to come.

It was a simple enough thing to do; though it's possible that even this experienced speaker had to steel himself a little to do it. Now you may well say that such a trick requires a degree of confidence that you do not (as yet) possess. Perhaps.

The point is first to recognize the effect of such a thing, and secondly to show that it is actually quite simply achieved. What had to be done took only a moment and a minimal amount of preparation (not least so that the notes actually needed were not destroyed), but it clearly reflected a state of mind – someone determined to be confident and to show confidence.

Who knows, by Saturday's chapter you may see such a thing as routine.

The results of lack of confidence

Let us be clear here too about the effects of a low level of confidence. First, it is uncomfortable, at worst even crippling, in an overall sense. It is to be avoided as it can be a continual factor reducing any satisfaction your job may provide and giving rise to feelings of stress (which in turn can lead to an ongoing negative cycle: low confidence makes you stressed, being stressed, or rather failing to cope with stress, makes you less able to be analytical and actually tackle and reduce the problem and so on). It handicaps your operating efficiency and spoils and interferes with everything you try to do and from which you should get satisfaction.

Secondly, it has specific effects: that is it prevents you getting to grips with individual tasks and executing them as well as you could if your confidence was higher. Have you ever had an interview, for instance, that worried you, went less well than it could have done and which, if you think about it honestly, went by default? In other words, you effectively gave up on it and did not really give it your best shot.

Lack of confidence is a tangible thing. It can be all pervasive, creating feelings of:

- Lack of enthusiasm
- Tiredness
- Shame, or even guilt or anger
- Sickness: headaches or stomach problems
- Inappropriate introspection and avoidance of people and situations

- Poor self-esteem
- Inappropriate compliance
- Poor concentration and focus
- Stress and anxiety.

All such feelings can affect your performance. Confidence affects your well-being and it cannot be left to find its own level, rather it must be seen as something requiring active attention. The question is how to address it.

TIP

If you recognize yourself from the list above then acknowledging that such symptoms may be linked to or stem from an insufficient, and perhaps, inappropriate, level of confidence can be a constructive first step to making a positive change.

The causes of a lack of confidence may be many and varied and range from childhood influences, experiences in the past (however far back) and relationships with others (including such extremes as bullying, harassment or rejection). Even physical personal characteristics may play a part. I once had a participant on a presentation skills course who was convinced their small stature prevented them from making a good job of this task, yet once they had some instruction and some practice, it quickly became apparent that this was no handicap at all and presenting was something at which they could excel. A change of perception may be all that is necessary in such a case.

The psychology of such past influences is rather beyond the brief here. A solution is more likely to be possible through *practical* intervention in the present than in deep analysis of the past. There is an old maxim that 'given oranges the job is to make marmalade'; the job here is to find ways to boost confidence regardless of such long-term influences. As the presenter described above found, acquiring a sound knowledge of how to go about making an effective presentation was far more important that a deep-seated fear that shortness of stature prevented doing such things well.

Routes to boosting confidence

Lack of confidence can result, in part at least, from natural human instinct and responses. Boosting it means resisting these pressures and taking steps which lead to you adopting a positive attitude to things. There is sadly no instant magic formula; confidence does not appear in a moment just because you punch the air and shout 'Yes!' On the other hand, there is a formula that does result in increased confidence, even if it needs working at progressively in a number of different ways. Be reassured, the effects of such working are cumulative. Remember the old (Chinese) maxim that a journey of a thousand miles begins with a single step. Each of the many things you can do to help your situation can act to boost your confidence just a little, until you might surprise yourself by the difference you have made.

At this stage it is useful to identify the main areas from which help can stem. Overall there are three:

1 *Consideration, attitude and understanding:* perhaps the foundation to change is to accept that change *can* be made. It is a prime aim of this book to help you adopt an attitude towards confidence of being able to work to increase it, and for you to see that the route to this is to think the problem through analytically (helping yourself to understand the problem) and select and take practical and specific action that will help.

2 *Focus on the task:* much lack of confidence occurs in relationship to specific tasks: a fear that if you lift the telephone to make that call, stand up to make that presentation or whatever you will be in trouble. As will be made clear, understanding the task, having sufficient knowledge about it and developing a suitable level of skill to do it, is a prime route to boosting confidence. Knowledge is power. So is proven skill, and thus there are some tasks where, realistically, confidence only truly builds with practice. Again, I repeat, confidence may not be raised instantly; some things are best dealt with through a campaign of confidence building. Realism about this helps the process: seeing yourself as taking useful steps, rather than despairing because confidence levels are not yet as you would wish.

3 *Feedback:* this also takes a number of forms. First, there is your own experience. Probably we have all had the experience of doing something for the first time (midst fear and trepidation) and finding it was not so bad after all, or even that it goes well. This certainly means we approach it differently the next time; when we *know* it is not as bad as we first thought. Secondly, there is the input of others, ranging from detailed help and advice about how to achieve something, to a simple word of encouragement. The latter is a good example of the power of small elements to add positively to the situation; again, surely all of us can remember a word of encouragement that helped us in some way. Encouragement, let me say, may be wholly pleasant, but it may also be incorporated with some authority and insistence (even with some power you may regard at the time as unpleasant). For example, your boss may tell you to get on and do something in no uncertain terms (leaving no possibility to say that you would 'rather not'), yet they may still include a strong element of encouragement, making it clear that they believe you are well able to complete the task successfully.

TIP

Another problem can be an overall fear of failure: we focus on the bad result, rather than thinking about how to achieve a good result. Think positive.

We return to these themes as the book progresses. Here let me add an analogy intended to make it easier to appreciate how a variety of things can help as you read on. Imagine your level of confidence represented by a set of scales. On one side are negative factors that pull your confidence down, on the other are positive things that act in some way to boost it. You want the plus side to weigh heaviest. Making this so can be achieved either by adding things: imagine them represented by plus signs of different sizes and weights, or by removing things from the minus side of the balance. Note too that a difference can also be made by reducing the weight of minus factors, rather than removing them, and similarly by increasing factors on the positive side; also note that small changes may affect the overall balance significantly for good or ill. This latter point means that small factors can be significant and must not be overlooked.

TIP

If you take just one thing from this chapter, let it be that levels of confidence can be changed, increased, and resolve to do just that, albeit step by step.

Summary

Thus the confidence building game-plan, as it were, is clear: you need to believe you can positively influence your level of confidence and construct an appropriate balance, going about that in a way that allows you both to assess and understand the problem and work to make things better. Another factor helps: that of understanding your starting point; seeing how you approach things now (and how you *are* now) will make the path to progress easier. It is to this we turn in the next chapter.

SUNDAY

MONDAY

TUESDAY

WEDNESDAY

THURSDAY

FRIDAY

SATURDAY

Fact-check (answers at the back)

1 Is level of confidence:
a) Fixed for life ❏
b) Always changeable ❏
c) Rarely changeable ❏
d) Only changeable by chance ❏

2 Is level of confidence most influenced by:
a) Being born confident ❏
b) Early experiences ❏
c) Working at being confident ❏
d) Good luck ❏

3 Which is the greatest influence on your confidence to perform a specific task:
a) Your knowledge of *how* to do it ❏
b) Your feeling about its difficulty ❏
c) The colour of your eyes ❏
d) Your experience of other things ❏

4 Lack of confidence can make you feel:
a) Content ❏
b) Hungry ❏
c) Lacking concentration and focus ❏
d) Uncaring ❏

5 Feelings of stress are most likely to:
a) Increase confidence ❏
b) Reduce confidence ❏
c) Not affect level of confidence at all ❏
d) Affect confidence very little ❏

6 Overall confidence can most easily be increased by:
a) Making one massive change ❏
b) Proceeding step by step ❏
c) Doing nothing ❏
d) Making one tiny change ❏

7 There are three areas from which a positive change can flow, which of the following is *not* the foundation for change:
a) Focus on the task ❏
b) Feedback ❏
c) Consideration, attitude and understanding ❏
d) Avoiding the full moon ❏

8 What imagined device can help you envisage your state of confidence and how it can be changed:
a) A saucepan ❏
b) A frying pan ❏
c) A kettle ❏
d) Weighing scales ❏

MONDAY

A little judicious self-analysis

In this chapter, we look at the overall influences that affect your level of confidence and see how understanding them can assist you. This book takes a practical approach to boosting confidence, not least because the focus is on the workplace and workplace-related tasks, so we will not get overtly psychological about things, though in a sense psychology is involved here.

Thinking through your situation (and indeed contemplating the kind of person you are), may well be helpful, but soul searching is no panacea. There are practical actions to be taken too, both to influence your thinking and to tackle and change other influences.

SUNDAY
MONDAY
TUESDAY
WEDNESDAY
THURSDAY
FRIDAY
SATURDAY

Consider first three overall factors that influence how confident you feel:

1 *Your background:* it is possible that attitudes which now dictate how confident you tend to feel (and indeed how you view life) link back to childhood and family circumstances. And it is also possible that any significant difficulties you have suffered in the past (and I mean a range of serious issues such as bullying or abuse) influence you too. Substantial problems of that sort are beyond the scope of this book, and some could need serious intervention. At another level such things may simply need leaving behind, and doing so may need only a small degree of resolve or a change to habitual thinking; after all you may conclude that some such matters have little link or relevance to your present day circumstances and activities. Of course there can be serious issues, and I have no wish to suggest such things do not exist, but it is all too easy to allow background issues to become an excuse (something you quote to yourself to excuse your lack of confidence rather than taking a view that can increase it). Writing this reminds me of a T-shirt I saw with the slogan *Yeah, right – move on.* Certainly that is a sobering reminder that other people may not be interested in, or make excuses for, your background problems.

2 *How you think:* a constructive attitude here is important. Faced with difficulty you need to think positively, and also to be realistic and practical as you may need action to overcome or reduce the problem. As has been said, the first thing here is a resolve to make a difference; more of this anon.

3 *What you do:* leaving a feeling of low confidence unaddressed (perhaps viewing it as inevitable or unchangeable) will achieve nothing. Some, often much, of what you can actually *do* will change how you feel about a task; although all fear of it may not be removed, you can make it possible, manageable, and even enjoyable (well, perhaps enjoyable having *done* it). Subsequent chapters focus on this approach, giving ideas and examples of how you can actively affect matters.

SUNDAY
MONDAY
TUESDAY
WEDNESDAY
THURSDAY
FRIDAY
SATURDAY

TIP

The best way to 'think positive' is not to dwell on the past, but to think analytically about factors that specifically prompt your current fears, and let seeking and finding solutions to them give you a positive boost.

If you aim to change yourself, or at least the way you feel about something, it is helpful to work out what degree of change is necessary. What is the starting position and how do you move from one condition to another? A little self-analysis is useful here.

Reversing negativity

Everyone surely has some inner self-motivation, sufficient to give them enough confidence to get out of bed in the morning and get down to the everyday tasks that face them (if you do not then this is not the book for you and you should seek more radical remedies). But confidence can be stillborn. You could be confident (perhaps you even feel you could be) but any such feeling is constantly overruled by negative thinking. This can take various forms, but all can be reduced or overcome. Consider the following factors.

Setting, and avoiding, 'impossible' tasks

This is characterized by taking an extreme view: feeling something is right or wrong, good or bad and so on. It is thinking that gets you setting your sights too high, believing something is only any good at the extremes, then avoiding getting started because you think *I'll never get there.*

Solution: Do not fix on an unmanageable whole, target. You must do it in stages (manageable stages). Make a start, work progressively through them, and congratulate yourself on successful completion (stage by stage). Right, a reward for me when I finish this chapter!

Allowing negatives to pervade thinking

This is an extreme form of the natural human tendency for negative self-talk. It can certainly be applied to a task like making a presentation, where you dwell on all the difficulties but forget any positives (you have to speak on something people will find interesting, you know the topic well, etc.)

Solution: Form the habit of assessing things in two columns, the plusses as well as less good factors; ask others about things too (perhaps picking the brains of one of your habitually more optimistic colleagues).

Jumping to conclusions

This reflects the term self-fulfilling prophesy: you find yourself habitually *sure* you know the key thing about something and that it is negative – like *knowing* the group will hate your presentation (but why should they?).

Solution: Look for evidence of your feeling. Is it a factual point or just a feeling? Again, a conversation with others, asking – *What's most important about this?* – may help you to adjust your focus.

Underrating your achievements

Belittling your actual achievements (and yes, I bet you have many) can easily be a habit of people with low confidence – and doing so just makes things worse.

Solution: Recognize what you do here and progressively aim to change this habit. Write things down, tell others what you have done (and listen to what they have done too) and mark achievements by giving yourself a metaphorical pat on the back or an actual reward (though not *too* much cake!).

Putting up a sign

Some people label themselves. They pick labels that demonstrate their low confidence: *I'm new to this job* (even after a few years) say or, worse, labels such as *I'm a disaster* (i.e. expressing the belief that nothing goes right, when surely much does). Psychologically having such descriptions in mind leads to negative thinking and thus to low confidence.

Solution: Ask yourself what you actually mean when you do this. Saying *I'm an idiot* may only mean you have made one minor slip and have nothing to do with the big picture.

Making mountains

... out of molehills. This form of overdramatizing is usually somewhat emotional – distress and drama escalate so that the perceived problem seems to way outstrip reality, and certainly prevents you from thinking logically about something.

Solution: Count to ten before you even begin this process, then you can spot the emotional self-talk as it comes to the fore. Remember that it will all be the same in a hundred years and that even if something is going to be difficult it may not be true to say it is an unredeemable catastrophe.

Making feelings facts

Here you let your feelings influence you, despite the fact that they are just your feelings. Thus being apprehensive about making a presentation does not mean you are less able to make one than other people, that's a view of yourself that *will* make it more difficult.

Solution: This thinking must be replaced by a more factual approach – asking *why* you fear doing something and then addressing the problem; it's another habit to establish in the right way.

Wrongly taking the blame

You should not take the personal blame for every problem or failure. Things can fail for all sorts of reasons, if you miss an important appointment because you let the car run out of fuel, then it may well be your fault. But if someone runs into you through no fault of your own, it may still leave you with problems to sort out but it does not help to blame yourself. Feeling bad about it won't help sort things out.

Solution: If something isn't your fault, don't beat yourself up over it. If blame is really shared (and this may need some assessment) then the responsibility for taking action to sort things out may also need sharing; again something to look at pragmatically.

This, therefore all

Here you allow one thing to be generalized. You make a pig's breakfast of one thing then apply it to everything. Not so. Say I write an unintelligible sentence, there is no need for me to feel the whole chapter is rubbish.

Solution: In my example, the unintelligible sentence needs sorting, and I need to keep this in proportion, not lose faith in the whole text. Again, like all these points, the key thing is to recognize what is happening, resolve another way is better, and change perspective. There is in fact nothing complicated about the solutions.

If you are to think positively and boost your confidence, then you need to consider how confidence originates. This is influenced in a number of ways.

Taking an initiative

There is a saying that if we want to do something we do, and if we don't we make an excuse. If a lack of confidence means we do nothing then, by definition, nothing happens. Allowing fate to guide us – a kind of 'something will turn up, let's wait' attitude – is a recipe for failure.

A first step is always to resolve not to dwell on something, but rather to actually tackle things (even if in so doing you also resolve to find out the best way of approaching it first).

Attitudes to success (or failure)

Think about something you have done: learning to ride a bike or drive a car perhaps. Almost certainly there was a stage where it just seemed impossible, but a degree of perseverance got you there in the end.

However, if you continued to feel it was impossible, gave up, assumed mistakes or setbacks meant you couldn't do it, blamed something (or someone) else for the difficulty or found endless excuses – then difficult or impossible it no doubt was.

But if you were prepared to invest some time, to try and try again, believed you could learn from your mistakes and get it right in the end, checked the best way to go about it and took responsibility for your actions – then you would likely have found it easier.

TIP
Never forget that your attitude directly affects your achievement – and that a positive attitude towards getting things done gives you the confidence to achieve.

Response to failure

Failure may just be finding the first stage of something uncomfortable and then backing off, but bouncing back is a better attitude. Avoid despair – *I'm useless, I'll never do it* – and recognize that the (initial) failure is less significant than your response to it. It is not just a question of try, try again; Henry Ford said that failure was an opportunity to start again *more intelligently.* The moral here is to confront the problem, consider the best way forward and make sure you expect future success. Viewing life as a series of opportunities to learn is an attitude that works well.

Optimist or pessimist?

It is said that some people see a glass as half empty but others, more positively, see it as half full. Maybe a better response is to say that the glass is simply the wrong size! Optimism is an aid to confidence, but it should not be based on unthinking faith in the future, rather it is based on an essential pragmatism and realism. Winston Churchill said: 'A pessimist sees the difficulty in every opportunity; an optimist sees the opportunity in every difficulty'. True enough: the confident approach rejects pessimism – an irrational *I know this will be difficult, I know I can't* approach – and sees success as possible, resolving to make it happen and, if necessary, to find out just how that can be made possible.

TIP

Most often lack of confidence persists because no effort is made to change things. Remember that if you always do what you have always done, things will tend to continue in the same old way. Change is inherent to building confidence. If how you are and how you think now leaves you lacking confidence, then you need to think and act differently.

Summary

The key issue here is how you think about things. Low confidence breeds even lower confidence all too easily. If there is one thing to emphasize about this, it is that many of the things referred to in this chapter are habits. We do not study the situation and then ignore all the positives, thinking this is the best way forward; rather we act instinctively and from habit that takes us in the wrong direction. Habits are not necessarily easy to change, but it is easier once you have decided what to aim to stop and what to put in its place. Then, progressively, you can find that good habits develop that are as powerful as the old, and that these will keep you on the right track.

At the start of this chapter it was said that the most important two things were how you think about things and what you do about them. Some of the soul searching you are aiming for in this chapter is important. Certainly just

SUNDAY

MONDAY

TUESDAY

WEDNESDAY

THURSDAY

FRIDAY

SATURDAY

knowing that there is an inherent artificiality to your low confidence – *it's only how I think about it* – helps. There are specific mental attitudes to address, but there are practical reasons underlying why it may be difficult to be confident about something. So now we turn to this, because focusing on solving difficulties and how you think at the same time can work wonders.

Fact-check (answers at the back)

1 Lack of confidence should be:
a) Ignored ❑
b) Addressed positively ❑
c) Recognized as 'just one of those things' ❑
d) Addressed primarily in the past ❑

2 Change should be regarded as:
a) Likely to exaggerate low confidence ❑
b) The final straw ❑
c) An opportunity ❑
d) To be avoided ❑

3 Optimism:
a) Has no relation to confidence ❑
b) Can be encouraged and used to combat low confidence ❑
c) Is an unchangeable personal characteristic ❑
d) Makes low confidence worse ❑

4 Your previous success (and surely there is some):
a) Does not mean anything will go well ❑
b) Means you are now due failure ❑
c) Can be used to encourage future success ❑
d) Has no relevance ❑

5 The prime route to boosting confidence is:
a) You taking the initiative to positively affect it ❑
b) Doing nothing ❑
c) Therapy ❑
d) Waiting for an outside input ❑

6 When things go wrong it is usually the fault of:
a) You ❑
b) Your boss ❑
c) A mix of circumstances ❑
d) Gremlins ❑

7 When you do achieve something, you should:
a) Regard it as a fluke ❑
b) Think of it as a minor matter ❑
c) Not dwell on it at all ❑
d) Give yourself credit ❑

8 Low confidence is often prompted by problems, these should be:
a) Addressed practically to seek a solution ❑
b) Ignored ❑
c) Regarded as insoluble ❑
d) Seen as unimportant ❑

TUESDAY

The nature of the workplace

The workplace is the stage on which you perform as it were. It can be a daunting environment, but also a supportive one. It can sap your confidence, or see it stifled, but it can also boost it in a variety of ways. Ensuring that you survive and prosper, and that you are able to undertake confidently the various tasks you must perform and perform successfully, means understanding the nature of the workplace and how you can use the way it works to assist your endeavours.

In this chapter, the workplace is explored to seek opportunities for boosting confidence. Some are very much part of ongoing activities, some need more effort to set them up, but there is considerable support available here. As has already been emphasized, the first step is a positive outlook. In some ways, you may see the workplace as one cause of you having insufficient confidence. Of course, there are difficulties and some are outright hazards, but the net effect should be positive. There is a real opportunity to pile things on the positive side of the scales here, and in supermarket jargon 'every little helps'.

In the 21st century we must all be realistic about the modern workplace. As Richard F. Stiegele said: 'The business world is an extension of the kindergarten sand box – but with quick sand'. The workplace has changed radically in recent years; if one wants one word to describe it, then dynamic is as good as any. As the 21st century moves on, any individual is right to wonder how their career will progress, and whether they can make it give them what they want.

Success in the workplace may have many influences, but the strongest is that success is based on the achievement of goals. And achieving goals may sometimes involve you in tasks that tax you and which you may feel little confidence in being able to do well. Furthermore, the workplace is increasingly competitive and if you do not have the confidence to forge ahead, then there will certainly be others who do.

Many people, certainly those with several years' experience, may feel they remember 'better times', that is times when there was more certainty about how a career would progress. Many organizations commonly once had defined career paths for people and, although progress varied somewhat, once on a specific path the direction in which you would be able to go was reasonably clear. In some industries this was particularly so. Banks make a good example, yet banks have changed too, more than many kinds of organization and, many would say, not for the better. Now, though this kind of prescribed career path does still exist, it is less common.

Some people may hanker for a return to these 'better days', but waiting for things to return to normal is simply not one of the options. There are currently few, if any, safe havens, and few, if any, organizations that seem likely to be so again in a situation where change is the norm. Organizations are always likely to be under pressure and the well-being of their employees, perhaps especially one whose lack of confidence does not help them shine, is often a lesser goal than sheer corporate survival.

All sorts of factors contribute to there being a different workplace and work culture today than in the past:

- Organizations being under greater market and financial pressure
- Changes in the way business and organizations operate (think of the IT revolution or international pressures, for instance)
- Lower staff numbers and more pressure on individuals
- Reduced budgets and thus a reduced ability to fund personal development
- Changed terms of employment (think of how the pension schemes offered have changed in the last few years)
- More competition between employees to succeed
- Higher unemployment
- A general increase in both the amount and speed of change
- The greater likelihood of employers having to take sudden and negative action to protect themselves (such as making people redundant).

Despite all this you no doubt want to thrive, prosper and get on; and ideally you probably want to enjoy your job while you do so. And remember, it is said that if success was easy, there would be no such thing as failure. So what is the moral? How can you ensure that you do well? The simple answer is that there is nothing you can do that will *guarantee* success (if there ever was). But there is a great deal you can do to make success more likely, ranging from learning new skills to surviving the office politics of a large organization.

Actively increasing the chances of doing well, by ensuring that your confidence is at a good level may be a crucial part of this. The concept of ensuring that your confidence levels are an *active* process is vital. For the most part, success does not come automatically to those who sit and wait, nor even to those who take advantage of opportunities as they occur, though this should be part of it. So too with confidence; brooding about your lack of it, or just worrying about whether you can cope with some task or not will not help. So let's see what there is about the workplace that can help.

Who's who and how they can help (or hinder)

People characterize the workplace. And, as has been said, the advice and encouragement of others can certainly boost your confidence. Essentially the categories of people that matter here are:

● Colleagues
● Your line manager
● Other managers

Let's take these in turn.

Colleagues

Let's get the bad news out of the way first. Some people will never help you. Remember that the workplace is hectic (so they may not have time) and competitive (so they may not want to help you, at worst they see themselves better off if you fail). This needs saying, yet actually because most people need help to some degree, and you are all thus as it were in the same boat, collaboration and good will are often in evidence in plenty.

The key is in the fact that you are not alone and it may be that you can prompt individual initiatives by offering help. Maybe someone is struggling with something that you regard as entirely straightforward. Offer help, and perhaps even arrange it as a swap: 'One gets so close to these things you can't see the wood for the trees, if I check over that report for you, perhaps you could spend five minutes making some suggestions about the presentation I'm preparing'. Even if you are terrified of making the presentation, you don't need to say that (though, if you know the person well you might), but just when you are convinced that your every planned word is useless it may be a boost to your confidence to have someone else critique it and find it mostly fine. If they can help improve aspects of it, then better still.

Relationships with colleagues may just sort of develop: but can usefully be guided so that they foster mutual support. Sometimes this mutual support may be practical. You might suggest a better way of starting a presentation, one that you find yourself using that makes you feel more confident. Alternatively, it may be simply a morale booster. For example, in the film *The Lady* (which tells the story of the Burmese pro-democracy leader, Aung San Suu Kyi and her husband) as Aung San Suu Kyi is sucked into taking a public stand, she must make a speech. Tens of thousands attend and, as she mounts the steps to the platform, she hesitates, pointing out to her husband that she has never spoken in public before. He directs her up the steps with a firm 'You'll be fine.' And of course she was, though I bet those three words were a powerful help.

Assistance of this sort, either just an encouraging word or sound advice, that makes something seem more possible and less worrying, works well. When it does, it is easily recognized, encouraged by both parties and becomes a useful routine. It is wise to regard such things as two-way, which is why a swap arrangement is good. You do not want to become known as a nuisance: someone always wanting help, perhaps help others feel should not be necessary.

 TIP
Relationships with colleagues is sometimes seen simply as what circumstances dictate. A consideration of the possibilities, coupled with some action to create the right involvements, can see you in a much more supportive group and gaining in confidence as a result.

Your line manager

A manager is responsible for ensuring that members of their team perform satisfactorily. Part of that may be checking on process, but it should also involve other things, primarily here motivating people so that they *want* to perform well and developing them so that they *can*.

A good relationship with a good manager is invaluable to your job satisfaction and level of confidence; I would go so far as to say that if you work for the 'boss from hell', working with the confidence you want may always be difficult, if not impossible. At worst you may resolve to move away from such a boss. That said, for most people, it is worth taking an initiative to create the kind of relationship with your boss that will be supportive and allow them to act to encourage you in a way that builds your confidence.

There needs to be a sound basis – a routine and a structure – if such a relationship is going to be constructive. This premise is easy to adopt, but then, unless your boss does all the work and creates exactly what you want, it demands two things of you:

1 *That you think the relationship through. You* need to take the initiative and think about what factors constitute a sound working arrangement. You can do worse than list them.
2 *That you make it happen.* Again, where necessary, take the initiative for creating and agreeing the appropriate basis, albeit step by step – and making it stick.

Any shortfall here will dilute your ability to succeed; if you cannot get precisely the arrangement you want first time (and this may well be the case), then you need to keep working at it.

Amongst the things that help this process are to:

● Adopt a day-to-day routine, especially with regard to how you communicate and how and when you have meetings; this is an element of good time management (something else perhaps worth some study, it does not help your confidence if you are forever struggling to keep up).
● Ensure regular communication (of all sorts, but especially meetings) and ensure you have sufficient time together to agree matters between you
● Make sure that project timing is agreed, and particularly that check points or progress meetings are scheduled in advance (by stage if not by date).

- Agree also the nature and style of all the above: for example, what exactly is a progress meeting? How long is it likely to take? Should it be preceded by a written document of some sort and if so what level of detail is involved?
- Make sure that such practice relates appropriately to tasks (that it is what is needed to get the job done) and to the people (so that both parties feel comfortable with it).
- Address both long and short-term issues. Think about what is needed day-to-day, right through to annual matters (like planning or regular job appraisal meetings).

It is important to relate all this to the nature of work and tasks. A progress meeting on an essentially routine matter may not take long or involve anything complicated; though it may still be vital to keep things on track. At the other end of the scale, a meeting that is designed to be creative – discussion that aims to identify new ideas or methods – will take longer and is also more likely to be squeezed out by matters that somehow have more immediate urgency. The routine should help make all things happen effectively.

Describing such a good working methodology is one thing, achieving it may well be another. Certainly it will not just happen (unless you have an exceptional manager), or will not happen consistently. So you need to be prepared to think it through, and see organizing how you work with your boss as something else on which you must be prepared to take an initiative. Thus:

- **Ask:** Ask for the opportunity to discuss things, and have some ideas ready (with a less approachable manager start just on one issue, a project perhaps, as a way of creating good practice).
- **Suggest:** Put forward ideas, offer suggestions, and use what other people (chosen because they will be respected) do to exemplify your case. Discuss, negotiate, request a test (plead?) – but get something agreed, even if it is at first a starting point that you return to, and refine later to move nearer to the ideal.

- **Action:** Take the initiative and act assumptively. In other words just do it. For example, as a project starts set out a timetable for scheduling the progress meetings and send it without comment, put (or through a secretary get put) the date in the diary, send an agenda ahead of the due date and appear ready for the meeting. Taking such action (assuming it is sensible and will be approved) makes sense; your boss may actually find it useful (maybe to the surprise of you both!) and not only react positively, but also react well to similar things in future.
- **Match their style:** Finally, as you approach all this, bear in mind the kind of person they are. What will suit them? Aim high by all means, but, if ultimately some compromise is likely to be necessary, plan what you might do. For example, attitude to detail is important here. Your manager may be a 'put it on one page' kind of person, or want every 'i' dotted, and every 't' crossed. You cannot just ignore such characteristics; a well-matched case has the best chance both of being agreed – and of working.

 TIP

Start as you mean to go on, suggest something practical, act to get it agreed and make it work so that your boss will want it to continue. Success breeds success, and confidence is fuelled by seeing the results.

Much here can act to boost your confidence. For example, embarking on a project when you have arranged some checks and opportunities to discuss it along the way, is very different to seeing the whole thing stretching in front of you and being uncertain about it. All occasions when you cross paths will present opportunities for you to seek information or simple encouragement. But remember that bosses want staff to be pretty self-sufficient. Saying 'I don't know what to do about X' and asking for help may not go down very well. Rather, make suggestions: 'I think the best way for me to do this is X' followed by checking to see if they agree, asking for advice about one aspect of the approach, or both. Make no mistake, a good, ongoing working relationship with your boss can improve both how you work and how much confidence you have in what you do.

Other managers

Similarly, it is worth thinking about other people in the organization with whom it might be beneficial (because they could provide help, advice or encouragement) to have good and regular relations. Who is appropriate will depend on the position you have and the sort of organization for which you work, but many staff managers can be useful, for example, a training manager. Again position what you do appropriately and so that you are not seen as inadequate, but rather keen to learn, develop, get on and do a good job.

 TIP
It can be useful here to make a list of all those you want to explore or maintain contact with, testing out who proves useful and keeping a simple record of contacts so that you establish a useful frequency (one that's not too much for others) and know when to make contact again.

One particular approach is useful here.

Mentoring

Encouragement breeds confidence and goes hand-in-hand with development. One source of it, beyond colleagues and your line manager, is a mentor. A mentor is someone who exercises a low-key and informal developmental role. Their role is to promote learning, but very much also to give encouragement and instil confidence. More than one person can be involved in the mentoring of a single individual. What they do is akin to some of the things a line manager should do, but a mentor is specifically *not* your line manager. Your mentor might be someone more senior, someone on the same level or from elsewhere in the organization. An effective mentor can be a powerful force in your development and success. So how do you get yourself a mentor?

In some organizations this is a regular part of ongoing development. You may be allocated one, or able to request one. Equally you may need to act to create a mentoring relationship for yourself (something that may demand some persuasion). You can suggest it to your manager, or direct to someone you think might undertake the role, and take the initiative.

What makes a good mentor? The person must:

- have authority (this might mean they are senior, or just that they are capable and confident)
- have suitable knowledge and experience, counselling skills and appropriate clout
- be willing to spend some time with you (their doing this with others may be a positive sign).

Finding that time may be a challenge. One way to minimize that problem is to organize mentoring on a swap basis: someone agrees to help you and you line up your own manager (or you for that matter) to help them, or one of their people.

Then a series of informal meetings can result, together creating a thread of activity through the operational activity. These meetings need an agenda (albeit just an informal one), but more importantly, they need to be constructive. If they are, then one thing will naturally lead to another and a variety of occasions can be utilized to maintain the dialogue. A meeting (followed by a brief encounter as people pass on the stairs) discussing a project, with a promise to spend a moment on feedback (an email or two passing in different directions), all may contribute. What makes this process useful is the commitment and quality of the mentor. Where such relationships can be set up, and where they work well, they add a powerful dimension to the ongoing cycle of development, one that it is difficult to imagine being bettered in any other way, and which, by their very nature, boost confidence too.

Overall, what you learn from the ongoing interactions and communications you have with your line manager and others can be invaluable. It may leave some things to be dealt with in other ways, but it can be the best way to cope with many matters, and also to add useful reinforcement in areas of development that need a more formal approach. As both parties become familiar with the arrangement, and with each other, it can become highly productive. Having been lucky enough to have someone in a mentoring role myself for many years, I well know that often just a few minutes spent together can crack a problem, lead to a new initiative or simply send you back to work more confident of what you have to do.

Note: a mentor is usually taken to be someone senior to the person for whom they act as mentor. But a similar relationship is possible with colleagues (for example, other members of your team or department). There is no reason why you cannot forge a number of useful and reciprocal alliances, perhaps each designed to help in rather different ways or on different tasks and topics.

TIP

In a good mentoring relationship it may well be that actually flagging a lack of confidence is a sound tactic and the mentor's reaction to this may well help. As this can seem like a display of weakness this needs some care but, successfully done, can pay dividends.

Mentoring is often an underrated methodology and is well worth investigating, experimenting with and using. The following section shows just how this can work and how useful it can be.

Mentoring in action

A mentor may act in various ways over time, but equally they may focus on a particular problem in the short term. Perhaps you could consider making another presentation. If you have to do one and dread it, then this may be an ideal topic for mentoring.

Once some help is arranged, and a promise to spend some time on it agreed, you can decide what to do and begin to set a timetable for it too (not least so that you always leave one encounter with the next defined, agreed and set in your respective diaries). Here you might start generally, the brief being that you need to know something about what makes a good presentation. In this regard you might:

- Read up on the subject
- Attend a course
- Talk through the essentials with the mentor (perhaps, to save time, having read a book first)
- Attend a presentation given by the mentor, with them meeting you afterwards, so that you could analyse it together and you could find out why different things were done the way they were.

Then you might link to your pending presentation:

- explain what it is to the mentor and discuss broadly how you will go about it
- prepare
- discuss the specifics of what you now plan to do and perhaps fine-tune it after some critique
- rehearse, then make the presentation to your mentor (and perhaps others), a session followed by a critique and perhaps again by more fine-tuning
- make the presentation (perhaps it could be videoed, or the mentor could sit in).

This is followed by a post mortem. This discussion will shape how you prepare your next presentation.

Of course, you may not follow this progression slavishly and could do more or less, but I am certain you will find that your confidence builds at every stage. The process is practical, it links to real life and a real project. You experience the progress you are making as you go through, with feedback contributing to your abilities and your level of confidence.

Setting things like this up right makes sense. It makes success both more likely and sooner than a more ad hoc approach, or one where you struggle to get through solo.

Summary

The workplace can seem hectic, confused and overpowering. An environment that crushes confidence rather than promotes it. And, unless considered and got to grips with, it is. On the other hand if you think about your position, if you are clear about what is expected of you in your job, and consider what and who can help make the path you must take a little easier, then there is much you can do.

The trick is to tackle individual elements separately and on a considered basis, rather than allowing the whole to overwhelm you. Thus organizing a good relationship with your boss (and working on it on an ongoing basis), finding and benefiting from a mentor and seeing who else might be useful, all help. There are things not to do also. For instance, not getting sucked into the less savoury aspects of office politics (which always exists in an organization of any size) or being seen as starting or passing on rumours.

Being well organized, managing your time effectively, focusing on the results

SUNDAY
MONDAY
TUESDAY
WEDNESDAY
THURSDAY
FRIDAY
SATURDAY

you are charged with producing, avoiding distractions and making sure you do not procrastinate (lack of confidence can easily lead to things being inappropriately put off) all help. It is doubly difficult to summon up suitable confidence when you are so submerged in chaos. You need to be thinking straight and knowing that you are actively organizing everything around you, so that it helps rather than hinders.

Fact-check (answers at the back)

1 The workplace is dynamic and this should be regarded as:
a) A passing phase ❏
b) Likely to continue ❏
c) Likely to continue and intensify ❏
d) Just an illusion ❏

2 Your manager is best regarded as:
a) Someone to avoid ❏
b) A potential help in boosting confidence ❏
c) Part of the 'low-confidence problem' ❏
d) Irrelevant ❏

3 Colleagues can help or hinder, so should be:
a) Avoided ❏
b) Cultivated carefully in terms of relationships ❏
c) Dealt with on a task-by-task basis ❏
d) Total confident ❏

4 In working with your boss, you should:
a) Just do as you are told ❏
b) Avoid discussions ❏
c) Ask questions and take initiatives ❏
d) Avoid them as much as possible ❏

5 A mentor can offer informal support, so you should:
a) Find and work with one if at all possible ❏
b) Regard this as 'not for me' ❏
c) Refuse any offer of such help ❏
d) Relate only to your immediate manager ❏

6 In the workplace you should:
a) Concentrate on your job and ignore things around you ❏
b) Observe and analyse your workplace for anything that will help you ❏
c) See it solely as a hindrance to your confidence level ❏
d) Leave any thought about it for later ❏

7 When dealing with staff managers (e.g. a training manager) you should:
a) Keep your head down and minimize contact ❏
b) Deal only with the 'business of the moment' ❏
c) Look for and cultivate useful inputs for the future ❏
d) Avoid contact with those outside your immediate circle ❏

8 A good tactic to obtain feedback and assistance from colleagues is:
a) Making collaboration a two-way process ❏
b) Becoming a real nuisance ❏
c) To limit what you ask drastically ❏
d) Forget it, it's not possible ❏

SUNDAY MONDAY TUESDAY WEDNESDAY THURSDAY FRIDAY SATURDAY

WEDNESDAY

Working at creating confidence

Three main routes to increased self-confidence include:

- the way you think about things
- the development of knowledge and skill
- addressing difficult matters in a practical, problem-solving way.

The latter, an area that links to the development of knowledge and skill, is the subject of this chapter.

If you are a sensible person (and why else would you be reading about this subject) you may say, okay I can sort problems; but you may still not be maximizing this approach. Joseph Jastrow once said: *Create a belief in a theory and the facts will create themselves.* This is so true of confidence. You become convinced that something is difficult just for some emotional overall reason (*I just can't do it*), and this belief allows you to avoid any analysis, and putting into effect any simple solution that might redress the balance, at least to some extent.

So let me encourage you to take a very practical view here.

Problem solve your way to confidence

The best way of demonstrating the possibilities here is through an example. I have already mentioned making a presentation and now, because so many people have to make them in their work (and almost everyone has experience or can imagine how easily lack of confidence handicaps the ability to make a good one), we'll use this as a good example. Of course, all sorts of things contribute to being able to make a good presentation, and preparation and a grasp of the 'tricks of the trade' as it were both help. To focus on matters that potential speakers rate as a significant contributor to nerves, consider the following common fears:

- butterflies in the stomach
- a dry mouth making it difficult to speak
- not knowing where to put your hands
- fear of the reaction of the audience
- fear of not having enough material
- fear of not being able to get through the material in the time
- not knowing how loud to pitch your voice
- losing your place
- over – or under – running on time
- being asked questions you cannot answer
- drying up.

All pose real hazards, but the way to deal with them, the way to ensure your confidence level is not affected by them, is to take a practical view. It is worth noting here that such fears are very often exaggerated. For example, last in the list above is drying up. Often during presentation skills courses, where usually I am using video to record what participants do and prompting discussion about it, people will regularly criticize themselves about one perceived fault: *I dried up at one stage*, they say, *there was an awful great gap*. Yet during their talk often no one noticed, except them, and often too when the video is replayed they cannot even spot where it happened. A pause just seemed too long to them at the time.

SUNDAY
MONDAY
TUESDAY
WEDNESDAY
THURSDAY
FRIDAY
SATURDAY

TIP

The preceding perception is very common. You may have fears about doing all sorts of things, but in all likelihood you see them as worse problems than they are; indeed, knowing you do so may help – in fact this alone may make you think of something that you can change.

Returning to the list, there are actions possible in response to all these points that actually sort out and remove the problems, or at the very least reduce them. For example:

Butterflies in the stomach: this is a physical manifestation of any worries you may have. In mild form it does no harm and fades as the adrenalin starts to flow when you get underway. On the other hand, a number of practical measures undoubtedly help reduce the feeling. Certainly, knowing a presentation is well prepared is a major help. Other things are seemingly small, perhaps obvious; they do work, however, and may work better when some are used together. They include:

- a few deep breaths just before your start
- no heavy food too soon before you start
- no starvation diets, or the butterflies will be accompanied by rumbles
- no alcohol (some would say very little) before the off.

Dry mouth: again this is a natural reaction, but one simply cured. Just take a sip of water before you start. And never be afraid of asking for, or organizing, a supply of water in front of you. Place it where you are least likely to spill it and you may, like me, prefer to avoid the fashionably fizzy waters supplied by many of the venues where speakers often find themselves, especially hotels and conference centres. I am sure it is nice for the audience and offered with good intentions, but it is inclined to make you burp if you are the speaker. The longer the duration of your talk, the more you will need to take the occasional sip. Talking makes you dry and air-conditioning compounds the problem. Act accordingly, throughout your talk.

Somewhere to put your hands: because somehow they can feel awkward. They seem like disproportionately large lumps at the end of your arms. The trick here is to avoid obvious awkwardness: give your hands something to do – hold a pen perhaps – and then *forget* about them, though they should be involved in some gestures. Incidentally, it is best that a man should remember that while one hand in a pocket may look okay, both hands in pockets always appears slovenly.

Though there are similar points to be made right down the list of presentational fears set out earlier, this is no place for a complete run down on making presentations*

A fear analysed can be turned into a problem with a solution. However long a list of fears, it can usefully be viewed in this way. Doing so can produce a radical shift: first you are just reacting, perhaps blindly, to a fear; then you have worked out a solution to a problem that alleviates what you fear (either completely or partly). Not only does the tangible result – there being one less thing to worry about – help, there is psychological advantage too. Knowing you have sorted the problem, indeed knowing that the overall balance of positive and negative effects is now adjusted just a bit more in your favour, helps boost your confidence.

There is perhaps another level here, different from simply perceiving and solving a problem, and that is finding things that simply suit you and make you feel easier about something; what you might think of as personal comfort factors. Continuing the presentation example, I find I speak regularly from behind a standard height table. Fine, one of reasonable width usually gives plenty of room for notes, slides, projector and more. But if I lay any notes I have flat on the table, then I cannot see them clearly if they are in standard-sized type. I wear spectacles and have found that if I lay a good sized, hard briefcase on the table and put notes on that, just four to six inches higher, then I can focus at a glance and, from the perspective of the audience, do not appear to be looking down so much. It suits me, looks fine and is easy to arrange. Having this in mind I can walk into an unfamiliar room carrying a briefcase and I *know* this will help me to be comfortable. So too

---

*I have written about this in *100 Great Presentation Ideas* (Marshall Cavendish) but these few examples make a good point.

will choosing a good-sized font. Such thinking and practice is proven and works well, and again such things shift the balance just a little more in your favour.

Consider one more factor on my list of presentation hazards: that of not knowing how loud to speak. This may be a reasonable fear in a strange room, but you can test it. Ahead of the meeting, find someone to stand at the back and check how you come over, until you get the level right. In fact, a moment's thought shows that it is not really a very difficult problem. In other circumstances, if a single person came into the room from a door at the far end, you would probably speak to them naturally at just the right level. Try not to worry and just think of yourself as addressing the back row. One further thought about this. There is an apocryphal story of a speaker checking and asking an audience 'Can you hear me at the back?' The reply comes back 'Yes ... but I'm prepared to change places with someone who can't.' Now, this may not be fall-about funny, but I find bringing a humorous thought to mind in any kind of stressful situation can help.

TIP

TIP

Always try to turn a, maybe amorphous, fear into a specific problem. Problems can have solutions, and identifying and using those solutions can quell fears and boost confidence.

Overriding the uncomfortable

Everyone has some difficult things to do.

Take me: despite being, I like to think, knowledgeable about, and practiced in various areas of management and business practice, there are, I admit, some tasks where my approach falters. It is difficult to admit this (damn it, I have written a book about time management!) – but I have been known to procrastinate. Where does this happen most often? On examination that is easy to say: it is when something is not just potentially difficult, but when it is a particular kind of difficult – when it is actually *uncomfortable*. This may be conscious: for example, there are things about my computer skills that mean action is delayed – I *know* that my skills have gaps and am conscious that it is easy to get into deep trouble, yet I still fear the solution and have little confidence in it proving straightforward. Everyone probably has things that prompt such thoughts, and which make delaying action more likely.

So, difficulty can translate into lack of confidence and thus inaction, and difficulty plus an uncomfortable awkwardness produces a worse effect. Consider an example that affects many of those who manage others.

When performance is inadequate

Imagine: one of your staff is performing under par. This might be anything from not hitting sales targets to more minor matters; the details are unimportant. One thing is clear – it demands action. The rewards are considerable, let us say, and easily recognized. Dealing with it will produce more sales, higher productivity – whatever, depending on the precise details. Yet ... with such things there can seem to be many reasons for delay. We think (or rather hope) that matters will get better. We wait for other things: the end of the month (bringing further figures or evidence) or a forthcoming appraisal (which we know means we cannot put it off later than that). More than anything we blame other things. We are busy, we have greater priorities (really?), or, even less convincingly, we are sorting other problems – fire fighting.

It may be an uncomfortable truth, but the truth is we do not *want* to deal with it. We may be unsure how to do so, and the resultant lack of confidence breeds procrastination. More likely we *do* know what to do, but know it will be awkward or embarrassing to do so; this is especially the case in some circumstances, for example where people managed may be senior or experienced. Addressing it will take us into what we might call the *discomfort zone,* and we would rather distance ourselves, busying ourselves elsewhere (with something we tell ourselves is more important!) and remain safely outside this zone of personal difficulty.

TIP

The facts of the matter are often clear, and can usually be dealt with if things are addressed directly. With the right approach and knowledge that the problem can be sorted, confidence rises and a good job can be done (even though there may still be some discomfort).

Poor performance is a good example. It is important, yet it is not complicated. Continuing the example, consider: essentially only three options are possible, you can:

1 Put up with the poor performance, and allow it to continue (which is surely something no manager would defend or recommend)
2 Address the problem determined to cure it, persuading or motivating someone to perform better; or training or developing him or her to do whatever it is better if poor performance is due to a shortfall in or lack of some skill or competence
3 Conclude, perhaps after option two has failed, that they will never get better and fire them (or otherwise move them to other areas of responsibility).

Both options two and three may be awkward. It *is* embarrassing to tell someone their performance is unacceptable, and most people would find firing someone worse. So, confidence falters and action is delayed.

Recognizing reality

The situation described needs to be addressed head on. Any such situation is not a failing of logic, not a deficit of information or understanding, or anything else that mistakenly leads us away from the sensible and necessary course – *it is a personal decision: we put avoiding personal discomfort above sorting the problem and, very likely, delay makes the problem worse.*

Before you say – *But I never make that kind of decision* – consider further. If this thinking is partly subconscious – we lack the confidence to do something rather than being unable to – then that means we push it into the back of our mind, refusing to really analyse what is occurring, or simply allowing other activity to create a blinding smokescreen. Now, thinking more constructively, which elements of your work are likely to run foul of this kind of avoidance technique? Other examples include:

- *Raising a difficult issue at a meeting* it gets put off rather than risking controversy or argument
- *Cold calling* in selling (many of us should do more, but it is not our favourite thing)
- *Networking* sounds good: we all hope to meet people at that conference we attend, but then come out with one business card because we are *not quite sure how to approach people.* Worse the card is from whoever sat next to us, rather than for someone selected for a good reason
- *Follow up* is when someone, a customer or colleague, has said *I'll think about it* – how many times do we make one perfunctory phone call to be told they are *in a meeting*, then leave it so long that the moment passes because we are not quite sure what to say next time
- *Chasing debtors* we hate it, avoid it or do it half-heartedly and so cash flow suffers; yet we should all recognize that an order is not an order until the money is in the bank.

TIP

A word about the last of these (or things like it). Next time you have to make such a phone call, don't sit at your desk – make the call standing up. It may sound odd, but do not reject this idea, I promise you will find it easier to be more assertive. Not only is it easier, it just shows how mechanistic changes can improve confidence.

Such things are, to an extent, routine. Others may be more personal, linking to a particular skill or activity. For instance:

- Avoiding presentations, even when they offer promotional opportunity, because *It's not really my thing.* Ditto other things; writing reports seems often to be regarded similarly.
- Avoiding sitting on a committee where you might make valuable contacts because meetings are in the evening and *It's not fair on the family*, though it is contributing to the meeting you fear.

You may well be able to extend the list in both categories (be honest, only that makes the analysis useful).

Identifying opportunities

So, what do we conclude from this? There is a significant opportunity here.

You need to resolve to *actively seek out uncomfortable situations*. You need to see the discomfort zone as an attractive place to go. It is somewhere where you can use analysis to raise your confidence, so that you can take action and influence results, and often you can do so quickly and easily. Indeed having done so, you may well end up saying: *I just wish I had done that sooner.* Give yourself a pat on the back.

Summary

The moral here is simple: some things seem worse than they are, so assume that they are. Think about it (analytically) and you can identify the real problem, find a solution and be much more confident of taking action to surpass or remove the fear. Make this approach a habit and adopt a systematic approach:

- spot the areas needing attention, an analytical approach and action
- ask yourself why you are turning away from something and check specifically that it is not simply to avoid what will (apparently) cause some personal discomfort
- check that action is possible: do you know what to do? Do you have the skills to do it?
- will any information or skills gap, taking time so to do if necessary (this is usually time well spent, for example fire someone without checking out the employment legislation situation and you may make a small hole very deep); we return to this in Saturday's section

SUNDAY
MONDAY
TUESDAY
WEDNESDAY
THURSDAY
FRIDAY
SATURDAY

- programme action into your list of 'things to do' giving actions their true priority and do so having worked out what you have to gain (after all you deserve some motivation if you are going to choose to be uncomfortable)
- take the action and take note: when you solve a problem, give yourself some credit, learn from it for next time and watch your confidence build – *Good job!*

Make this approach a habit (and perhaps make *entering the discomfort zone* a catchphrase). This approach is the antidote to a lack of confidence which allows things to go by default. It needs some resolve, but surely you have that. Here is truly a technique which, simply by overriding an undesirable element of human nature, provides a simple, sure way to boost confidence, and thus increase your effectiveness and enhance the results you achieve. Try it. This approach works – and as you discover that, your confidence in the approach will rise.

Fact-check (answers at the back)

1 If a task fills you with dread, what's best to do?
a) Panic ❏
b) Blame ... anything ❏
c) Analyse the problem and seek a solution ❏
d) Hope someone else can assist ❏

2 Faced with a problem what does low confidence make you most likely to do?
a) You will ignore it ❏
b) You will overrate it ❏
c) You will underestimate it ❏
d) You will not notice it ❏

3 If you sort a problem, what (other than the solution) do you gain?
a) Brownie points ❏
b) A psychological boost (*I sorted it!*) ❏
c) Nothing ❏
d) Things get worse ❏

4 If a problem is especially *uncomfortable*, how should you approach it?
a) Delay any action to avoid the discomfort ❏
b) Just sit and worry ❏
c) Do something – anything – instantly ❏
d) Make sure you address it promptly and in a considered fashion ❏

5 What can change your attitude and ability to tackle something instantly?
a) Holding your breath ❏
b) A physical change (such as standing to make a phone call) ❏
c) Nothing ❏
d) Putting it out of your mind ❏

6 How will avoiding an issue because of lack of confidence affect things?
a) The delay won't matter ❏
b) I'll feel better ❏
c) It will guarantee nothing changes ❏
d) Something will turn up ❏

7 What analogy is useful in envisaging how problem solving helps boost self-confidence?
a) A microscope ❏
b) A telescope ❏
c) A set of weighing scales ❏
d) A calculator ❏

8 In the presenting example, what best helped the fear of knowing what to do with your hands?
a) Wearing gloves ❏
b) Putting your hands in your pocket ❏
c) Giving them something useful to do ❏
d) Making exaggerated gestures ❏

SUNDAY MONDAY TUESDAY WEDNESDAY THURSDAY FRIDAY SATURDAY

THURSDAY

The contribution of appearance

There is an old saying that if you look like a doormat, then people will walk all over you. And lack of confidence can show. People who appear to be lacking in confidence look uncertain, they look worried or worse. Such can create something of a continuing problem: people read a lack of confidence as a lack of competence. They treat people displaying it differently, and that in turn makes it more difficult for the person so treated to rise above the situation.

Thus how you come across to others is important, and so I have now included a chapter on how personal appearance affects confidence and thus performance.

It was Oscar Wilde who said: 'Only fools do not judge by appearances'. He was right. The first thing to take on board here is that how you appear (and as we will see it is more than just your personal appearance) is important. It makes a difference. Look confident and you will feel confident. Look confident and other people will rate your competence more highly. As they say in the world of advertising 'perception is reality'.

It is not difficult to do either; creating the right visible persona is thus a straightforward step to take. In terms of the balance mentioned earlier, it puts distinctly more weight on the plus side.

Making a judgement

Think of someone in your organization perhaps whom you do not know very much about. Ask yourself what you think about them. Are they busy? Competent? Confident? Approachable? Expert? Ambitious? Efficient? If they are a manager, what opinion do you think their staff has of them? You will find that if you draw conclusions from what evidence you have, many questions can apparently be asked and answered, and a reasonable picture builds up. You feel that you can judge something about them. Whether it is true or not is, of course, another matter. Your own visibility also gives out many signals, and will do so whether you think about it consciously or not. Here we review some of the ways in which you can give signals that paint the right kind of picture of you: as a confident and competent person. This will both be read by others and make you see yourself in a more positive way, to boost your confidence.

Look the part

I once attended an evening talk at a professional institute and heard someone give a review of what are sometimes called 'beauty parades' or competitive pitches. The speaker made a number of interesting points including the simple advice: look the part. He gave a number of detailed examples, one of which was the advice for men to wear what he called 'big-boy shoes' (ones with shoelaces rather than slip-on style). Now this is going a bit far perhaps, but the point is well made. First impressions, which of course can only be made once, are largely visual and take in many such things from clean finger nails to someone's overall prevailing style.

Now dress is a difficult area on which to advise precisely. I am not promoting designer fashion or any specific style of dress. You have to be reasonably natural, but you want to be seen positively. You can be smart without spending a fortune. You must always be clean and tidy, and the details matter. The Americans, who have a jargon phrase for everything, talk about 'power dressing'. This is a concept that is too contrived for many; indeed there is a real likelihood that going too far in this way becomes self-defeating, and is just seen as pretentious. It may be important in some jobs to meet the standards and style of those with whom the organization does business rather than internally. Once having met with a major bank to discuss possible training work, a colleague of mine, one who took a pride in his appearance, was dismayed that a letter came back requesting the work to be done by someone *shorter in the hair and longer in the tooth!* An older and more traditional alternative was found and the work went well; that is the client's right. Internally, styles vary in different organizations and types of job, and certainly dress codes are less formal than they used to be. Any variable may influence things: summer and winter, a totally internal role or one meeting customers, and geographic location (for instance business suits may not be worn in a hot country).

TIP

In terms of dress the best advice is to be towards the smarter end of the range exhibited by colleagues around you. Feeling you have this right, that you fit in and fit well, will be a foundation to feeling confidence in your appearance.

So, what specifically is certain? The following are often mentioned:

● Clean finger nails and tidy hair
● Smart (rather than over fashionable) clothes
● Clean shoes

And, though it is more difficult to judge, your appearance should reflect an appropriate spend; hence the comment in the 'Tip' above. It is worth noting that men and women have different styles to consider, with the greater choice facing the women, frankly making their choices more difficult. Whatever your style, whatever you opt for, think about it, relate what you do to the corporate culture and practice, and remember your appearance says very much more about you than you might think. You *will* have an image; the only question is what precise image you will make it.

Your workspace

The same principle applies to your desk or workplace. It should be tidy, it should look well organized, you should be able to find things promptly, and certainly, it should be uncluttered (not too many photos and probably no stuffed animals); and it should say to others: here works someone on top of the job, organized, competent and professional.

If your desk is an untidy muddle, if it looks as if a bomb hit it and you frankly have difficulty finding things, then remember the old saying that a tidy desk means a tidy mind. You may sensibly not want a look that seems to flag inactivity (there is nothing wrong with looking busy) but do consider this advice.

Have a tidy up, create a look you feel is appropriate, and you will not only feel better about it and yourself, but the picture you paint of yourself to others will improve. This simple act alone can boost confidence and begin to change any inadequate image that may exist. There is an important link here: changing things so that your appearance is strengthened can also act to change your view of yourself and how confident you feel. More is necessary, but this can be a positive step in the right direction. That said, what else can have this sort of effect? The following can be useful:

Body language

This has perhaps been over inflated in the way it is written about. It is not really a science, but at the basic level there are things here to note because they do signal something and you will want to control this.

Take two examples: we all know how we feel if we are given a really limp handshake, or if someone fails totally to make eye contact with us. Both are to be avoided. It is easy, if you are feeling a lack of confidence, to find yourself evading eye contact, but knowing it is important, surely helps. Make a point of meeting someone's eyes: they will judge you differently and as they do so you will feel better about yourself.

A conscious effort just to look more confident is worth some effort. Without it you become trapped in a downward spiral: your look says the wrong things about you and you are judged accordingly. This is especially important initially, on first meeting someone, at the start of a meeting, or the beginning of a conversation, interview or presentation. Remember that first impressions last and that you should start as you mean to go on. This is precisely the sort of area where making a good start is so important: you look someone straight in the eye, their respect for you increases, and you quickly see the benefit Later, such things become habits that need little thought.

Take an interest in your interests

In many companies, particularly large ones, there is considerable social interaction amongst staff. Just how much is there and how it works will vary, and is affected by such things as whether there is a social club and where the office is located: some city centre locations where people typically travel long distances to work may mean people live as much as a hundred miles apart and this will reduce social possibilities. It is easy if you lack confidence to avoid all of this, but that is almost certainly a mistake.

There will also be a culture within the organization relating to this kind of activity. In some companies, senior people are involved in some of this and others are clearly expected to be. In others, it is seen as a lower level activity and you may not want to get too involved, in case you are seen as essentially frivolous.

Another issue here is that, rightly or wrongly, people have a total image. Though interference in employees' private lives is not the style of many organizations, and would be resented by many staff, you may be expected to have certain interests. Some of these are perfectly reasonable. It is useful for executives, especially those who have contact outside the firm, to be generally well-informed in terms of current affairs, for example. If you are in a technical area, you may need to keep up-to-date on a broad range of scientific matters, simply to be able to relate well to others you work with. On the other hand, there are organizations where the style of the chief executive – evidenced by a passion for, say, golf, science fiction or undersea diving – is mirrored by aspiring staff around the office forever plunging into the sea or Arthur C. Clarke. Whether this last is useful or not is uncertain. I would like to think it is not, but there are organizations where this kind of fitting in is important. It is certainly worth a thought. You are unlikely to have to rearrange your whole life around such things, but some accommodation with such perception may be useful.

 TIP

Taking steps to become socially comfortable within the workplace, and finding that you are, is a direct boost to both self-confidence and how you are seen. Avoiding contacts and events, not because those things are difficult, but because you are embarrassed about a poor presentational ability say, just makes things worse. Aim to move forward in parallel: tackle the specific problems and you will not have anything standing in the way of fitting in.

Sex

Fear not, this section will not provide a guide to your love life. It is here for two reasons. First, because the conventional wisdom of publishing is that any book that is seen to refer to sex will sell more than one that doesn't! And, more seriously, because the gender of any individual inevitably has an effect on how they are seen. This is no place for a major debate on women in business; suffice it to say that they are still, in many cultures, not taken as seriously as men. Leaving the reasons on one side, what is the effect? Let me start with an illustration. I used to have a young lady working with me who moved from a secretarial position to one of more executive responsibility, and then to a position where she joined a small management committee. Halfway through the first meeting she attended, someone delivered a tray of tea and coffee and left it on a side table. Discussion continued and, after a few minutes during which no one moved, she got up, poured and handed round the drinks.

After the meeting, she asked me how she had got on. She had done well, contributing some sound comments, but I remember asking, *'Why did you pour the tea?'* She did not hesitate, saying at once, *'Right, I won't do that again.'* Now I am not suggesting that every woman early in a management career is in danger of being typecast as the tea lady, or secretary/hostess, and it did not in fact matter who did the chore, the point is that perceptions stick. Sometimes women are in danger of being underrated and thus, rightly or wrongly, they have to think twice as hard as a man about how they are seen. So in my view, her response was right (and her subsequent progress proved she made sure that she was very much seen in the right light). Of course, women can increasingly fight their corner, and I like the quotation, attributed to (a presumably confident) Charlotte Whitten: Whatever women do, they must do twice as well as men to be thought half as good. Luckily, this is not difficult. Even so, this area may need some conscious thought.

Similarly, and for everyone, there is merit in making sure all dealings around the organization are on the basis of jobs done, expertise and merit rather than gender (whichever gender is involved). I do not suppose anything I might write will prevent the occasional normal social interaction, and in organizations the world over, some people will continue to have the confidence to say: *How about dinner?* Back to business.

Do not drink in excess

This is common sense, but worth a word. A lack of confidence can lead in this direction; a stiff drink before you must make that dreaded presentation say. In many organizations, a certain amount of socializing is not only pleasant; it is also part of the way the business works. On the other hand someone being the worse for drink gives few, if any, confidence in them and most, if not all, managers will always prefer to promote the office cat before promoting someone with even a hint of a drinking problem. Enough said.

Give and take

Beware, a lack of confidence can promote a selfish outlook and think of the effect a selfish attitude in others has on you. It is not the most endearing characteristic imaginable. Success and effectiveness is assisted by cooperation. Liaison with others has been mentioned elsewhere, and a selfish attitude to others hardly makes them cooperate in ways that will help you become more confident (that is a forgone conclusion).

When I first went into consulting, I worked with a group of people who were less selfish than any other I have encountered before or since. No one ever seemed too busy to help. You could walk into any office and get advice, information and support of all kinds – from just a word to a complete run down on something (and if it could not be given at once a time was set). Information was regarded as for sharing, not for exclusive hoarding, and the whole firm, far from grinding to a halt because time was taken in this way, seemed to thrive on the attitude. For a newcomer, it was a godsend. I made full use of the learning, accelerated experience and greater confidence it provided and, in due course, found myself part of the network spending time giving as well as receiving.

There is an altruistic side to this attitude. You never know in an organization how things will go and how things will turn out. The person whose head you bite off because they want a moment of your time when you are busy, turns up a while later in a position of authority or influence, and with not the slightest intention of sharing anything with you. You cannot have too many allies; contact and collaboration is a prime source of increased confidence and being seen to be involved in this kind of way is a positive image factor.

Avoid being typecast

Every kind of business activity seems to run this risk. In my own business, it is very difficult to stop some clients seeing me exclusively as a consultant, others seeing me exclusively as a trainer or a writer (though I work at it!). Some companies have a similar problem in selling the range of what they make; they are known for one, or two main items, and the others always seem to get left behind. There can be a similar situation with people and sometimes the effect can be negative.

For example, if a lack of confidence in the past has seen you hiding your light under a bushel, failing at some tasks and avoiding others, then there is a danger that, well let's just say you are not the first name to jump into the bosses' mind when some new and interesting project needs staffing. Image is part of the story, so too is your track record. There is a virtuous circle possible here. Look the part, and you will be taken more seriously. Being taken more seriously, perhaps being given new tasks you find you can excel at, changes your image still more, while fuelling your confidence level in the process. One good thing leads to another, and in terms of getting started, one small step forward can make sure the next one follows.

Create image opportunities

You may feel that your role within an organization is too low key ever to contribute very much to what you might call your corporate profile. If so, then one option may be to add opportunities. This may not be for everyone, but you could surprise yourself by examining what you could do. The following is a dramatic example perhaps, but it makes an important point.

Once waiting to do a radio interview, I remember meeting another interviewee who was there to comment on some technical matter. We got chatting and I asked him who he was. He said that he worked for a large company and had made a point of becoming known as the company's expert on the particular technical issue in question. *Do you run the technical department?* I asked him. *No,* he said. *But I aim to.* Hearing what he was doing to establish himself as the technical 'guru', I was inclined to believe him.

This tale makes a good point: public relations is not only a valuable tool to promote the company, it has personal development potential as well. It is tightly linked with some of the communications skills reviewed in the next chapter. My fellow interviewee at the radio studio would not have been there unless he could talk fluently about his chosen topic; just being knowledgeable about it was not enough. What is more, if he performed well, then he stood a good chance of being asked back, while his boss, who was fearful of undertaking the task, stayed in the office.

Radio is perhaps a dramatic example to take, though by no means unattainable, but public relations activity incorporates many different possibilities. Given that you have or can create some expertise worthy of comment, and very many jobs have this possibility, start internally. You review the possibilities, for instance:

● Is there a company magazine or newsletter?
● Are there groups or committees you can take part in or speak at?
● Should you be seeking to write articles?
● Can you speak at the local management institute or trade or professional body?

There may be many options, and this is very much an activity that creates its own momentum. If you lack confidence in meetings, perhaps you simply need more practice. Though it may be the last thing you believe you want, volunteering for a committee role may provide a useful low key introduction, in which you can experiment and build confidence for those meetings that matter more to you.

One such thing can lead to another, with your confidence building along the way. For example, an article published in the company newsletter might be adapted to go in an external publication, a copy of that being sent to a professional body might prompt an invitation to speak, and at that meeting you might meet some who ... but you get the point.

If such activity grows up naturally, and has a use for the organization as well as for you, then it should not create ripples (though others may well wish they had thought of it first) and it can become an ongoing part of how you signal to others that you are going places. Nothing succeeds like success they say, and being seen to have achieved things is certainly potentially useful. There is a chain of events possible here where each step can build confidence, and the success achieved step by step does the same. Before you know it, what you thought of as a lack-lustre image of someone unwilling or unable to say 'boo to a goose' can have been transformed. See you in the studio.

TIP

Personal image is not a given. You create it, wittingly or not, and you can build it into something that influences others and influences you too, making you better able to take on more because you believe you have the wherewithal to do so.

Summary

Be aware: every aspect of how you appear plays a role in how you are seen. As the examples here have shown, the range of things contributing to the overall picture is considerable (from how you look, to the state of your desk, and your manner when conducting a meeting); so it is worth some thought and some care to get this right.

The right personal profile – consistently – is important in a career sense and that may benefit you long term, but it is also something that you can draw strength from, so that your confidence builds (and is seen to do so) as the cumulative effect of a number of individual manageable actions.

Know the kind of profile you want to have, in detail, and work at everything that helps to create, maintain and project it. Why not start with a review of how your work area looks?

Fact-check (answers at the back)

1 Does appearance matter?
a) Hardly at all ❑
b) No ❑
c) Yes, it conditions your professional persona ❑
d) Very little ❑

2 How much do people infer from appearance?
a) Just what it obviously shows ❑
b) Very little ❑
c) Nothing ❑
d) Far more than it actually shows ❑

3 What else contributes to your visual profile?
a) The appearance of your workspace (desk or office, etc.) ❑
b) Keeping a low profile ❑
c) Wearing dark glasses ❑
d) Only communicating by email ❑

4 What easily positively boosts first impressions?
a) Your choice of tie ❑
b) Direct eye contact ❑
c) Speaking extra loud ❑
d) A painfully crushing handshake ❑

5 How will a stiff drink affect your confidence?
a) Not at all ❑
b) Likely to make things worse ❑
c) One isn't enough ❑
d) Boost it dramatically ❑

6 When is appearance most important?
a) On special occasions ❑
b) On Tuesdays ❑
c) Throughout working hours ❑
d) When the boss is around ❑

7 What forms an inherent part of appearance?
a) Nothing else ❑
b) Your behaviour and manner ❑
c) The car you drive ❑
d) Your favourite colour ❑

8 How often should you review and fine-tune how you appear?
a) Once a year ❑
b) Every five years ❑
c) Every time you look in the mirror ❑
d) Regularly, but without wasting time on it ❑

FRIDAY

Communication to the rescue

Think about this: how quickly and easily could you tell someone who doesn't know how to tie a necktie? And no, you cannot demonstrate – words only. Are you confident you could do it? No? Well, perhaps many would agree, certainly it would be difficult without some thought.

We all communicate, much of the time, and the workplace is no exception. Often all goes well. Often we hardly think about it. It's easy enough to say, 'What time do you call this?' to the postman but asking for a salary increase, making a presentation to the Board or writing a report that will actually be read (and influence a decision towards the one you want made) can be another matter.

Well, leaving aside the postman, the answer may be not only that such things can be difficult, but also that when they are poorly executed, problems can appear not far behind. In most workplaces you do not have to eavesdrop for long to hear the immediate results of poor communication: *But I thought you said ... You should have said ... What!?* Similarly failing to get your point across at a meeting or making a lack-lustre presentation can change the course of subsequent events – to your detriment. Here we review communications, recognizing that some, for instance presentations, are almost inherently confidence sapping, and that even seemingly more routine matters can be made difficult by a lack of confidence.

The fact is that communication is often *not* easy; indeed a host of factors combine to make it more difficult. And one such, without a doubt is a simple lack of confidence. You ponder and pause – *how can I put this?* – or you rush into something, quickly getting tongue-tied – *sorry, I suppose I mean sort of ...* Furthermore, such stumbling is highly likely to make you less confident: an awkward start deteriorating into self-talk that just says *I can't do this* and the avoidance of conversations that would in fact be helpful to you. Alternatively, if you assume all will be well, and give the matter no great thought or preparation, then of course the dangers increase. And, of course, any such stumbling risks you being taken less seriously by your peers and others; as the entertainer Tom Lehrer said *I wish people who have trouble communicating would just shut up.*

Hello, I must be going

One notoriously difficult kind of communication is indicated by the idea of networking, which is the work equivalent of joining a cocktail party where you know no one and are trying to think of something to say. At work it may literally be networking, trying to forge contacts at a trade conference perhaps, or just meeting any unknown group, attendees on an all-comers course, or just visiting a department or location of your own organization where you don't know anyone.

You want to feel fine not flustered, so the way ahead is to have a firm idea of how to handle the situation. How do you go about this? First, remember that this is a common problem and many people present are probably wondering *what do I say?* It is best not to interrupt passionate conversation, but easier to start a conversation with someone alone or just starting some small talk. Use the mnemonic FINE. It is most straightforward to talk about:

- **F**amily
- **I**nterests
- **N**ews
- **E**mployment

And it is easiest to make a start with open questions – that is something that cannot be answered with the words yes or no. The best start is with the likes of what, where, how, where and phrases like *Tell me about …*

Of course, it may still be difficult to steal yourself to take an initiative, but knowing you are on an easy topic and that most people like nothing better than to talk about themselves does make it easier. It may help to remember something like FINE, but so too does it to understand something about the psychology of communication.

In Roman times, Marcus Fabius Quintillian said:

> ### *One should not aim at being possible to understand, but at being impossible to misunderstand.*

Communication is, in fact, *inherently difficult*. However tongue-tied any lack of confidence may make you, understanding the difficulties and what makes it work well, enables you to position what you do correctly, and this alone makes things easier. Let's consider why.

The difficulties of making communication effective

If communicating is going to flow easily and make things happen, everyone must make sure that people:

- Hear what you say, and thus listen
- Understand, and do so accurately
- Agree, certainly with most of it
- Take action in response (though the action may simply be to decide to take note).

Such action could be a whole range of things, from agreeing to spend more time on something, attend a meeting or follow specific instructions.

Consider the areas above in turn:

Ensure people hear/listen (or read)
Here difficulties include the fact that:

- People cannot or will not concentrate for long periods of time: so this fact must be accommodated by the way we communicate. Long monologues are out, written communication should have plenty of breaks, headings and fresh starts (which is why the design of this book is as it is), and two-way conversation must be used to prevent people thinking they are pinned down and have to listen to something interminable.
- People pay less attention to those elements of a communication that appear to them unimportant: so creating the right emphasis, to ensure that key points are not missed, is a key responsibility of the communicator.

TIP
Always remember that you have to work at making sure you are heard – you have to earn a hearing. That it just how things are (it is not that people are being perverse, they are being normal!)

Ensure accurate understanding occurs

Difficulties here include the fact that:

- People make assumptions based on their past experience: so you must make sure you relate to just that. If you wrongly assume certain experience exists then your message will not make much sense (as was said earlier, imagine trying to teach someone to drive if they had never sat in a car: *press your foot on the accelerator – what's that?*).
- Other people's jargon is often not understood: so think very carefully about the amount you use, and with whom. Jargon is 'professional slang' and creates useful shorthand between people in the know, for example in one organization or one industry, but dilutes a message if used inappropriately. For instance, used in a way that assumes a greater familiarity than actually exists it will hinder understanding (and remember, people do not like to sound stupid and may well be reluctant to say – *I don't understand,* something that can apply whatever the reason for a lack of understanding).
- Things heard but not seen are more easily misunderstood: thus anything that can be shown may be useful; so too is a message that 'paints a picture' in words.
- Assumptions are often drawn before a speaker finishes: the listener is, in fact, saying to themselves – *I'm sure I can see where this is going* – and their mind reduces its listening concentration, focusing instead on planning their own next comment. This too needs accommodating, and where a point is crucial, feedback can be sought to ensure that concentration has not faltered and the message really has got through.

Prompting action

Often this is an objective and one you must aim for, despite the fact that:

- It is difficult to change people's habits: recognizing this is the first step to achieving it; a stronger case may need to be made than would be the case if this were not true. It also means that care must be taken to link past and future. For example not saying: *that was wrong and this is better* – but rather: *that was fine then, but this will be better in future* (and explaining how changed circumstances make this so). Any phraseology that casts doubt on someone's earlier decisions should be avoided wherever possible.

- There may be fear of taking action – *Will it work? What will people think? What will my colleagues think? What are the consequences of it not working out?* And this risk avoidance is a natural feeling: recognizing this and offering appropriate reassurance is vital.
- Many people are simply reluctant to make prompt decisions: they may need real help from you and it is a mistake to assume that laying out an irresistible case and just waiting for the commitment is all there is to it.

In addition, you need one more objective:

Stimulating feedback

The difficulties here are that:

- Some (all?) people, sometimes deliberately hide their reaction: some flushing out and reading between the lines may be necessary
- Appearances can be deceptive. For example, phrases such as *Trust me* are as often a warning sign as a comment to be welcomed – some care is necessary.

The net effect of all this is rather like trying to get a clear view through a fog. Communication goes to and fro, but between the parties involved is a filter, not all of the message may get through, some may be blocked, and some may be warped or let through only with pieces missing. In part, the remedy to all this is simply watchfulness. If you appreciate the difficulties, you can adjust your communication style a little to compensate, and achieve better understanding as a result.

TIP

If you know that every utterance you make is likely to be met with confusion, antagonism or just ignored, then it hardly acts to boost your confidence – if you know the likely difficulties, and know how to work to overcome them, then your confidence benefits.

One moral is surely clear. Communication is likely to be better for some planning. This may only be a few second's thought – the old premise of engaging the brain before the mouth (or writing arm) – through to making some notes before you draft a memo or report, or even sitting down with a colleague for a while to thrash through the best way to approach something.

There are antidotes hinted at above to these inherent difficulties, but are there any principles that run parallel and provide mechanisms to balance the difficulty, and make matters easier? Indeed there are.

Aids to effective communication

Confident and successful communication comes largely from attention to detail. Just using one word instead of another can make a slight difference. Actually, just using one word instead of another can make a *significant* difference (as you see!). And there are plenty of other factors that contribute, but there are also certain overall factors that are of major influence, and which can be used to help your communications.

Four factors are key:

1. *The 'What about me?' factor*: Any message is more likely to be listened to and accepted if how it affects people is spelt out. Whatever the effect, in whatever way (and it may be ways) people want to know *what's in it for me?*, and also wonder *how will it hurt me?* People are interested in both the potential positive and negative effects. Tell someone that you have a new computerized reporting system and they may well think the worst. Certainly their reaction is unlikely to be simply *good for you*, it is more likely to be *sounds like that will be complicated*, or *bet that will have teething troubles or take up more time.* Tell them they are going to find it faster and easier to submit returns using the new system. Add that it is already drawing good reactions in another department. Spell out the message and what the effects on them will be together and in the right sequence, rather than leaving them wary or asking questions.

SUNDAY MONDAY TUESDAY WEDNESDAY THURSDAY FRIDAY SATURDAY

2. *The 'That's logical' factor*: The sequence and structure of communication is very important. For example, if people know what your proposition is, understand why it was chosen and believe it will work *for them*, then they will pay more attention. Conversely, if it is unclear or illogical then they worry about it, and this takes their mind off listening. Something like this book makes an example: it might be possible to have a chapter investigating the fundamental principles of communication, such as Chapter 1, and a reason for it; but I doubt it. Certainly readers would query it and look for a good reason.

Information is remembered and used in an order – you only have to try saying your own telephone number as quickly backwards as you do forwards to demonstrate this – so your selection of a sensible order for communication will make sense to people, and again they will warm to the message. Using an appropriate sequence helps gain understanding and makes it easier for people to retain and use information; as with much of what is said here this is especially true for a technically orientated or complex message.

Telling people about this is called *signposting*: Flagging in advance either the content or nature of what is coming next; one important form of this is describing a brief agenda for what follows.

Signposting is a very useful device. Say – *let me give you some details about what the reorganization is, when the changes will come into effect and how we will gain from it* - and, provided that makes sense to your listener, they will *want* to hear what comes next. So tell them about the reorganization and then move on. It is almost impossible to overuse signposting. It can lead into a message, giving an overview, and also separately lead into sub-sections of that message. Sometimes it can be strengthened by explaining why the order has been chosen – *let's go through it chronologically – perhaps I could spell out …* – within the phrase.

TIP

Whatever you have to say, think about what you say first, second, third and so on and make the order you choose an appropriate sequence for whoever you are communicating with. You will gain confidence from the certainty of having this worked out.

3. *The 'I can relate to that' factor*: Imagine a description: *it was a wonderful sunset*. What does it make you think of? Well, a sunset, you may say. But how do you do this? You recall sunsets you have seen in the past and what you imagine draws on that memory, conjuring up what is probably a composite vision based on many memories. Because it is reasonable to assume that you have seen a sunset, and enjoyed the experience, in the past, I can be fairly certain that a brief phrase will put what I want in your mind.

It is, in fact, almost impossible not to allow related things to come into your mind as you take in a message (try it now: and *do not* think about a long, cool refreshing drink. See.) This fact about the way the human mind works must be allowed for and used to promote clear understanding.

On the other hand, if you were asked to call to mind, say, the house in which I live and yet I describe it to you not at all, then this is impossible; at least unless you have been there or discussed the matter with me previously. All you can do is guess, wildly perhaps – *all authors live in a garret – all authors are rich and live in mansions* – (and here this is wrong on both counts!).

So, with this factor also inherent to communication, it is useful to try to judge carefully peoples' prior experience; or indeed to ask about it if you have not known them for long and you are unsure of their past experience. You may also refer to it with phrases linking what you are saying to the experience of the other person. For example, saying things like – *this is like – you will remember – do you know so and so? this is similar, but* – all designed to help the listener grasp what you are saying more easily and more accurately.

TIP

Beware of getting at cross purposes because you think someone has a frame of reference for something which they do not; link to their experience and use it to reinforce a message in which you can have greater confidence.

4. *The 'Again and again' factor*: Repetition is a fundamental help to grasping a point. Repetition is a fundamental help to ... Sorry. It is true, but it does not imply just saying the same thing, in the same words, repeatedly. Repetition takes a number of forms:

● Things repeated in different ways (or at different stages of the same conversation)
● Points made in more than one manner: for example, being spoken and written down
● Using summaries or checklists to recap key points
● Reminders over a period of time (maybe varying the method: phone, email or meeting).

This can be overdone (perhaps as in the introduction to this point here), but it is also a genuinely valuable aid to getting the message across, especially when used with the other factors now mentioned. People really are more likely to retain what they take in more than once. Okay, enough repetition.

Positioning your communication

So far in this chapter, the principles outlined have been general; but they can be useful in any communication. However, exactly whom you communicate with is important. Consider staff, reporting to a manager, as a special category. If you want people to work willingly, happily and efficiently with you, one useful approach to any staff communication is to remember not to allow your communication style to become too *introspective*. If you want to influence them, then relate to them in a way that makes *them* the important ones. Although you speak *for* the organization, staff members do not appreciate an unrelieved catalogue, which focuses predominantly on your side of things:

- the organization is ...
- we have to make sure ...
- I will be able to ...
- our service in the technical field is ...
- my colleagues in research ...
- our organization has ..., and so on.

Any such phrases can be turned round to focus on the people, thus:

- you will find this change gives you ... you will receive ... you can expect that ....

A slight mixture is, of course, necessary, but a predominantly introspective approach always seems somewhat relentless. And it is more difficult when phrasing things that way round for you to give a real sense of tailoring what you say to the individual: introspective statements sound very general. Using the words *you* or *yours* (or similar) at the start of a message usually works well, and once this start is made, it is difficult for you to make what you say sound introspective.

Summary

Any difficulties with communication, and the lack of or negativity of response that goes with them, quickly has you feeling inadequate. You should take comfort from the overriding truth that communication is *inherently* difficult (it is, just listen for a while to any group or around an open plan office). If you stumble because you do not really understand the fundamental details of why this is so, and what in fact can help make communications flow smoothly, then do not knock yourself out – just resolve to learn more about it.

The other truth flowing from the inherent difficulty of communicating is that doing it successfully needs some thought (remember the old saying about engaging the brain before the mouth and some planning (though for many purposes that only means a moment's thought). Which of us has never dashed off an email without thinking and then regretted it? No one, I bet. Yet often the difference between what falls on stony ground or actually causes upset is just a little thought and a few words differently selected.

SUNDAY

MONDAY

TUESDAY

WEDNESDAY

THURSDAY

FRIDAY

SATURDAY

Almost always the emotional fear that can stop you even trying to communicate (as with asking for a pay rise or sorting out a difficult relationship) is not rational. It is more likely that you do not know the best way of asking the boss for more money, rather than that you do and do so badly.

Again the route to success is often just thinking about what the problem really is and searching for a remedy. Given the 'to and fro' immediacy of much communication, the trick is not to rush in, but to deliver only a considered message and, as it said on the cover of *The Hitchhikers' Guide to the Galaxy* 'Don't panic!'. Too often people rush into saying something instantly when there would be no harm at all in saying 'Let me think about that for a moment'. In the moment that follows, you may be surprised how much consideration your brain can bring to the matter.

Knowing that you understand communication in a way that will help you do it successfully, will itself give you confidence.

Fact-check (answers at the back)

1 What is the main reason communicating is difficult?
a) It presents inherent difficulties (that can be negated) ❏
b) I am inherently bad at it ❏
c) Actually, it's easy ❏
d) People don't like me ❏

2 What topics make networking conversations go best?
a) Religion ❏
b) Politics ❏
c) Death ❏
d) FINE: family, interests, news and employment ❏

3 Why is getting people to pay attention difficult?
a) They are not interested in me ❏
b) They are not interested in what I say ❏
c) Paying attention is inherently difficult (and can be combatted) ❏
d) They are just perverse ❏

4 What will most readily boost confidence in communicating successfully?
a) A stiff drink ❏
b) Understanding (and using) the psychology of communication ❏
c) Not doing it ❏
d) Shouting ❏

5 Communicating is made easier by what?
a) Speaking off the top of your head ❏
b) Putting your message over at great speed ❏
c) Thinking (preparing first) – engaging the brain before the mouth ❏
d) Being extremely brief ❏

6 How can you make things clearer?
a) By signposting what is to come ❏
b) Through sign language ❏
c) By using lots of jargon ❏
d) By constant repetition ❏

7 What sort of logical sequence works best?
a) Alphabetical order ❏
b) Largest to smallest ❏
c) A sequence chosen to make sense to the other person ❏
d) Random ❏

8 Which word, used regularly, enhances good communication best?
a) Me ❏
b) You ❏
c) The organization ❏
d) Them ❏

9 Which statement is the truest?
a) Emails are quick and easy to use ❏
b) Emails are damaging to communication ❏
c) Emails should always be well-considered ❏
d) Emails can use mainly standard phrases ❏

10 What's a good phrase to use to buy some thinking time?
a) Hold on, not so fast ❏
b) Let me think about this for a moment ❏
c) I must go to the bathroom ❏
d) ·Or, just pause ❏

SUNDAY

MONDAY

TUESDAY

WEDNESDAY

THURSDAY

FRIDAY

SATURDAY

SATURDAY

A foundation of knowledge and skill

Whatever you must do, it has been made very clear earlier that a prime promoter of confidence is that you know you have the knowledge and skill to do it. This has been shown through example and is something surely that every reader can relate to from their own experience. For example, driving a car is certainly a complex skill, and if you can do this, I bet you went through a stage of virtual despair when you were convinced that you would never get everything that must be done co-ordinated together. Yet, millions of people move past that stage and drive successfully – once they know what to do and have sufficient practice.

Because an utter lack of confidence to do something can be done away with, transformed into comfortable performance, and even with much that needs to be done relegated to habit (though please drive carefully!), you need to both assess your skills and take action to acquire those you need, and then keep up to date. This needs some thought and some initiative. Knowing how much it can improve your confidence must be an incentive.

In this last chapter, it should now be clear that a good understanding of something, then developed skill in doing it, is the best confidence builder of all. Getting and remaining in this position is an ongoing process, as Henry James said *Experience is never limited, and it is never complete.* To pursue this thought, you need to assess how exactly your development should proceed. Doing this, and implementing a plan flowing from the analysis, can prove to be one significant, ongoing confidence building exercise.

It is worth thinking this through in a systematic way and, of course, doing so honestly; deceiving yourself and ignoring gaps in your knowledge or skills will not help either performance or confidence. First, you should remember that development can only do three things:

● improve your knowledge
● develop your skills
● change your attitudes.

With that in mind, consider the thinking involved as a ten-step process:

1 *Identify the requirements of your present job in terms of knowledge, skills and attitudes* – you need to be honest about this and think broadly about it (and it is clearly easier if you have a precise job description).

2 *Identify your own current level of such knowledge, skills and attitudes* – look at how well you are currently equipped to perform in the job.

3 *Identify any additional factors indicated as necessary in future because of likely or planned changes* – in today's dynamic business climate there are likely to be some of these.

4 *Consider and add any additional aspects that a long-term view demands* – this can look as far ahead as you wish, but realistically should concentrate on the short/medium term.

5 *Set priorities* – note what needs to be done, there may well be more than it is realistic to change very quickly and you then need to set clear priorities to help you make progress; in this context things linked to your greatest lack of confidence rank high.

6 *Set clear objectives* – always be absolutely clear what you are trying to do and why.

7 *Consider the timing* – in other words, when any development might take place, and this in a busy life means one thing at a time, and perhaps at a slower pace than you would ideally like.

8 *Implement* – do whatever is necessary to complete the development involved. This could be very simple: you doing something that you can control. Or it could involve discussion and debate with others (e.g. your line manager) to get agreement about the need, and to committing the necessary time and money (for instance, to attend a course).

9 *Evaluate* – this is important. Many people forget to really think through how useful and relevant something, like attending a course, has been. A little review can ensure much better linking to your real job and make future tasks more manageable.

10 *Assess against the job/career factors* – as well as evaluating general usefulness of anything done, it is useful to match its effect on both current tasks and future career plans.

Then you are back to the beginning again. The process is a continuous cycle, something where regular review is necessary, if not month by month then certainly year by year. Next, you need to relate this to a plan and then think about the actions that are implied to see it through.

Have a self-development plan

In today's dynamic world, development must be a continuous process. There will be new skills you need to acquire during your career and perennial skills to be kept up to date. If you are with an organization that has a sound development policy, the thinking needed here may well be prompted by what action is available for you. If not, or if what is done is (in your view and for your needs) inadequate, then you will need to initiate more. You need a plan. Not something cast in tablets of stone that stretches into the future and is unchangeable, but a rolling plan, something that sets out immediate actions or intentions clearly, and an outline for the longer term. The detail of this will have to change as events unfold, and you must adjust to changing circumstances and needs. To relate this to the example of presentation, to help with this and boost confidence too, you might:

- Read a book about it
- Request and arrange to go on a course
- Arrange to do more (yes, for practice)
- Work with a mentor to help your preparation and evaluate your progress (refer back to Tuesday).

Just knowing you have some of this arranged, and believing it can boost confidence (even ahead of the development activity taking place) will help.

When you have thought this sort of thing through and made some commitments, trust your judgement. There is a lovely line in the film *Loch Ness* when the monster-hunting scientist tells a little girl claiming to have seen the famous beast that he'll believe it if he sees it. No, she tells him, you can only see it if you believe. Trust your judgement – believe what you have arranged *will* help and your confidence can get an immediate boost.

The options in terms of action are several:

- The organization may suggest something (e.g. attendance on a course)
- You may want to suggest something to them
- You, or they, may want to amend or adapt an original suggestion
- You may conclude that whatever the company does, you will do more to meet your own personal objectives, including working in your own time.

The permutations are, of course, many. The key thing is that you regularly devote a little time to considering what you feel would help (for example, the company will be more inclined to spend money on things that have a reasonably short-term impact for them, while you may want to look further ahead).

There is an important link here with any company job appraisal (or performance assessment) scheme, which you find yourself taking part in – many organizations have their own schemes. Some consist of just an informal annual meeting. Others are more formal and more regular. Such schemes, if they are good, are very much to be commended and, well handled can be a catalyst to both development and raising confidence. After all, the focus of an appraisal should be on making things go well *in the future*. They offer an opportunity to link your personal plan with that of the organization for which you work. With the support and approval of your immediate boss, you will probably find you can do more that will benefit your current job (and the tasks it entails) and help yourself proceed more confidently into the future as well.

Having a development plan really works. Creating and maintaining one should not be regarded as a chore. If you take a moment to keep your thoughts straight about this area, you will be able to action more of what you want, and better able also to take advantage of circumstances. Consider more about some simple development options.

Read a business book; regularly

As I make my living, in part, by writing, this may seem like a plug, but this is certainly amongst the simplest forms of development and a good deal can be learnt from it. It takes some time, but is also something that you can allocate to certain moments when perhaps time would otherwise be wasted. Such time includes travelling; and I know more than one salesman who always carries a business book to read in those; sometimes long, moments he regularly spends in his customers' reception areas.

The first rule is to make it a habit. Always have such a book 'on the go' (even if it takes you a while to get to the end) and keep watching for what is current in bookshops, by reading the reviews in the press and getting yourself added to publishers' mailing lists.

The kind of book to concentrate on is one that links directly to your development need, like *How to write a report* or whatever. Your choice here may reflect immediate needs or something you wish to develop for the future. Remember, it may be useful to come at things in different ways. Constructive repetition will help you take in the message, so it is worth reading more than one title on certain topics. Other more general titles may be useful too, but informing yourself about something specific that you need to build up confidence about should be the priority.

This may seem a small point, but applied conscientiously its effect may be considerable. A book every quarter, for instance, is still quite an input of information over say five years of your career. Six a year is better still, and you can apply the same principle to a range of things from technical journals to websites.

Attend a course

Courses, seminars, workshops – whatever word you use – can be very beneficial. Do not regard attending as a sign of weakness or be embarrassed about it. Remember that a group attending a course are all in the same boat and all want to know more about the topic. And in the long run, spending a couple of days on such an event is not too high a price to pay compared to what may be gained from them. Some employers will regularly give you the opportunity to attend both external courses or those set up and run only for their personnel. If not you may want to prompt them. If you are making such suggestions, particularly to attend outside events, remember you must put your case persuasively. Just ask to attend, even if some of the thoughts that come to mind may be negative: *That's expensive* or *Once they have extended their skills a little more they will be likely to leave the organization.* So, tell them what *they* will get. Explain what more you will be able to do for them and for the organization; will you be more effective, more productive, and better able to save or make money? If so, explain how.

Choose carefully. If you make wild suggestions, something that clearly only benefits you in the long term, or ask to attend something every week, you are unlikely to get agreement. Make practical suggestions and get approval, and you perhaps create the right kind of precedent and habit. I remember once battling for three years for the budget and time to attend an annual conference in the United States. Once I had attended and it proved useful, then it rapidly moved to being a regular event. Certainly, the most important consideration is the course topic and content, but realistically there are other things to think about. Where is it being held, who is organizing it, speaking at it, and attending it?

One single new idea, or even one single existing idea (confirmed with sufficient weight to prompt you into action in some particular area), is all that is necessary to make this process worthwhile. At best, there is a great deal to be gained by it, with benefits going way beyond increased confidence. Under the next three headings, we investigate specific aspects of course attendance.

Getting the most from course attendance

It is said that you only get out of something what you put in. Certainly this is true of course attendance. First, once attendance is arranged, you should think through what you want to get from it. This will help you and the course tutor. I know my heart sinks if I ask people on seminars, which I conduct, why they are present and their only answer amounts to, *I was told to be here.* Never go to a seminar without a written note of your objectives and any specific questions you want to obtain comments on. Most trainers are happy to get a note of questions in advance, though in my experience this is rarely done. Such thought gives you confidence too, to ask something in front of a group; you will have thought it through and know it's a sensible point.

Thereafter, you need to think about how you will behave 'on the day'. If the programme is internal (in-company), you may know all the other participants and the whole tenor of the event may be informal. If it is external, it can be a little more daunting to arrive in a room of participants knowing no one. Everyone is in the same situation, however, and the informal contacts and the comments and shared experience of your fellow participants may be an important part of your attendance (this is essentially similar to networking, refer back to Friday). The checklist which follows sets out suggestions to course participants and makes, I think, some useful points about being open-minded and adopting an approach which is constructive. In view of the time and cost of attending such events, it is a great pity to walk away at the end with any key question still unanswered.

An example of a document issued to delegates at the start of a course (or ahead of attendance)

NOTES FOR DELEGATES:

This manual contains all the basic details of this training programme. Further papers will be distributed progressively during the course, so that a complete record will be available by the last session.

This is *your* seminar, and represents a chance to say what you think – so please do say it. Everyone can learn from the comments of others and the discussion it prompts.

Exchange of experience is as valuable as the formal lectures – but you need to *listen carefully* and try to understand other points of view if this is to work.

Do support your views with facts in discussion, use examples and stick to the point.

Keep questions and comments succinct – do not monopolize the proceedings, but let others have a say, so that various viewpoints can be discussed.

Make points in context as they arise. Remember that participation is an attitude of mind. It includes listening as well as speaking, but also certainly includes constructive disagreement where appropriate.

Make notes as the meeting progresses. There is notepaper provided in this binder. Formal notes will provide an aide-memoire of the content and coverage, so any additional notes should primarily link to your job and to action on your return to work. Even a few action points noted per session can act as a catalyst and help ensure action follows attendance.

A meeting with colleagues, staff or your manager on your return to normal working can be valuable. It acts as a bridge between ideas discussed here and action in the workplace, and can make change more likely.

It will help everyone present if you wear your name badge, respect the timetable, and keep mobile telephones and pagers switched off during the sessions.

This is an opportunity to step back from day-to-day operations and consider issues that can help make your job more effective. Be sceptical of your own operation, challenge ideas, remain open minded throughout, and actively seek new thinking that can help you to prompt change and improve performance.

Note: here also you may find listed any necessary 'house rules', the observance of which can improve the course experience for everyone attending.

It is important to adopt the right approach. Time at such an event goes all too quickly, and it is easy to leave and then wish you had had the courage to ask something else. Try not to worry about what people will think. Sometimes you may feel others are all ahead of you in understanding. Usually they are not. A question postponed, because it seemed obvious and likely to make you appear stupid, actually (once asked) can prove to be a common question, which can lead into a very useful discussion for all.

Maximize course attendance benefits

The most important thing about any course you may attend is what happens after it is finished. Courses may be interesting, they may even be fun, but what really matters at the end of the day is the action that they prompt. So even more important than the notes you make before attending, is the action plan you make afterwards.

Note, such a plan has to start at once. It is inevitably for most people that, if you are away for even a couple of days at a short course, you are going to have more in the in-tray afterwards than if you had not attended. Yet the moment to start any action resulting from the course is the following day. Nothing later will do. The likelihood is that you will get involved in catching up and everything will be put on one side and forgotten.

So whatever else you do, take ten minutes on the day after attendance to list – in writing – the areas of action you noted during the programme. At least get them on your 'to do' list, whether they are things to think about, to review further or to take action; whether they represent things you can implement solo or things you will need support or permission for and must raise at the next appropriate meeting. If you do this much, and then approach them systematically and with an eye on the priorities, something is more likely to happen. If you miss this stage, the danger is not that you will do less, but that you will do nothing.

TIP

Early action is easier too, because you will be more confident of something while it is fresh in your mind. Putting things off (perhaps through lack of confidence) just makes something more likely to be difficult.

So, follow up your notes, do not just have good intentions, but make firm action plans. Consider also:

- Review and keep safe any course notes that were useful.
- Have a de-briefing session with your boss, the training manager or whoever sent you. If they are convinced it was useful, then future requests may be that much easier to make and get agreed.

When you do this is worth considering. There cannot be much implemented action to report immediately, but your recall of the detail will be greater. Later on, you can review what you have done more realistically.

Thus two meetings may be worthwhile. If your company asks you to complete an assessment form about the course attended, always do so thoroughly and on time. They are useful to the process of deciding what training is used in the future. Not doing this may be seen as indicating you have no interest in training.

Just attending a developmental event is nearly always useful. If it is a well-chosen and practical one then it may be very useful; and if you go into the process with the right attitude and take the right action before, during and after the event, you will maximize the benefit that comes from it.

Continue learning – at a distance

Change, including technological change, affects almost everything in our lives; including education and training. What is called 'distance learning' is now widely available in many forms. This is a rather imprecise term that covers a range of rather different things, but the principle in all cases is similar – that of receiving some kind of formal training (including education resulting in a qualification) by working alone, linked to, but not actually attending, the establishment providing the tuition. These days this will often involve working online via the internet.

The options are many and varied, and allow you to study part time while continuing to work full time and develop your career on the job front. You can undertake anything from an MBA to a short course covering some individual skill area. The form of the course will include conventional study, with things to read, but may also involve a series of other methodologies: videos, exercises, programmed learning and, in the best formats, the ability to complete projects and papers that are sent away and then receive individual critique and comment to help you through the whole exercise. Some courses do involve some group activity. Weekend sessions are sometimes used to fit this aspect in, without making it impossible for those working full time to attend.

The area is worthy of some investigation for anyone wishing to extend their learning. But, a word of caution – because of the profusion of material that has become available, there is, amongst excellent material and schemes, some that is frankly not so good. A good deal of work is involved in any lengthy distance learning course, so it is worth selecting what you do carefully, and there are also considerable differences in costs.

 TIP
Having some continuing activity of this sort provides an ongoing confidence booster as you progressively work your way through something and benefit from so doing.

Take on new things

Make a point of taking on new things. Low confidence may steer you away from doing so, but experience and the range of your competence are both things that must be kept moving, like sharks which must keep swimming or sink. There is a temptation in many jobs to stick with the areas of work that you feel are 'safe', by which I mean where you do not have to stretch and where you are sure of what you can do. This is almost always a mistake. Allowing that if you spread your learning too wide you may end up with some expertise across too broad a front rather than a real strength in particular areas. However, an ongoing objective to broaden your range of skills, expertise and experience is likely to be helpful to you in the long run – a more confident and competent you.

 TIP
Monitor how this goes, record what you do and succeed at that is new. It can provide additional job satisfaction and your confidence will grow as you make doing so a habit – I did that okay, so now why not this?

You never know what the future holds and, at the risk of my sounding very old, it is an easy mistake when young to rule out possibilities on the grounds of some inherent prescience. I know from my own experience that skills that have helped me more recently in my career formed no part of my expertise early on; indeed some were things I feared. With hindsight, I do not think I always predicted what would be useful in this sort of way. So, next time something new is on offer, something that will stretch your powers and even where the outcome is somewhat more certain, think very carefully before you allow yourself to say *I can't*, decide to avoid it or say *no*. You could be taking on something that will kick-start your abilities and your confidence.

Summary

Development will not just happen. Take an initiative, base what you do on sound analysis and make it make a difference to your work, your confidence and even your career. In doing so, I believe that you will find the whole exercise confidence building in a number of ways. It is good to have:

- assessed your skills portfolio and know the state of play
- a plan of development activity on the go and in the diary
- plans to keep you up to date and help you tackle new things
- actually done and completed activities scheduled (albeit step by step)
- experience of having undertaken development of some sort that manifestly makes you able to tackle something with more confidence and do it better.

Every stage here can build confidence. It stands repeating: a prime cause of low confidence is a lack of understanding or ability. Usually both can be acquired and knowing that you have the necessary competencies is a solid foundation to

SUNDAY
MONDAY
TUESDAY
WEDNESDAY
THURSDAY
FRIDAY
SATURDAY

achieving what you want. Of course, even things you are familiar with may worry you to some extent. Boosting confidence may not remove fears, but it will reduce them and allow you to focus on the positive. For example, for all my experience with training and making presentations, standing up in front of a new group always has a daunting quality. A good start helps disperse it, so too does knowing that what you are doing is well prepared and deploys the techniques that make such a thing work well.

Whatever you must do, you will do it better, more easily and more confidently with a firm foundation of knowledge and skill. Recognize this fact, address the issue and your confidence will surely rise.

Fact-check (answers at the back)

1 What gives you confidence for many a task?
a) Knowing how to go about it ❑
b) Knowing little about it ❑
c) Guessing what might work ❑
d) Giving up before you begin ❑

2 What is the time scale for development?
a) Six months ahead ❑
b) An annual cycle ❑
c) A life-long process ❑
d) A moment now and then ❑

3 Significant useful formal development is possible on what?
a) Holiday ❑
b) A training course ❑
c) A train journey ❑
d) Wednesdays ❑

4 Added confidence is built through what?
a) Putting something off ❑
b) Practice ❑
c) Ignoring skill development ❑
d) Astrological prediction ❑

5 Progress is often best made in what way?
a) Stepping unprepared in the deep end ❑
b) Making a mountain out of a molehill ❑
c) By taking one step at a time ❑
d) Proceeding without thought ❑

6 How best do you maximize development time?
a) Just drop everything and do it ❑
b) Plan carefully and make use of flexible low-time methods (like reading a book) ❑
c) Accept that you just can't ❑
d) Alter your watch ❑

7 What's one thing that helps you get the best from a course?
a) Linking content and coverage to your needs ❑
b) Keeping quiet throughout ❑
c) Asking no question ❑
d) Ignoring other participants ❑

8 What attitude to new things helps build confidence?
a) They are to be avoided ❑
b) They are opportunities ❑
c) I should stick to what I know ❑
d) They should be ignored ❑

Postscript

So where are we? Looking back over the seven days, we have examined the business of confidence in various ways and there is only a single conclusion to be reached. Whatever level of self-confidence you have comes from you.

You make it happen.

That said, there are a variety of (largely practical) things that help you do this. Various factors can act to strengthen both the level of confidence you have and also the level it appears to be to others. To end, I believe an old traditional story strikes the right note:

In medieval times, a baker in the King's household found himself condemned to ten years' imprisonment for some small misdemeanour, burning a cake perhaps. Languishing in his cell, he thought about his plight and he sent a message to the King promising that, if he were released, he would work day and night in the Royal stables and, within a year, he would teach the King's favourite horse to talk.

This amused the King, and he ordered the servant to be released to work in the Royal stables. The servant's friends were at once pleased to see him released, yet frightened for him too; after all horses do not talk, however much training they get. 'What will you do?' they all asked. 'So much can happen in a year,' he replied. 'I may die, the King may die, or – who knows – the horse may talk!'

Who knows indeed; I'm sure he had no confidence in teaching the horse to talk, but he clearly saw it as a step forward (after all he was no longer in a cell). I for one hope that by the time the year was up he had thought of another ruse to take him forward. The tale makes a good point, well several good points that link to our theme:

● Thought, analysis (and perhaps creativity too) tend to proceed successfully making a change to your level of confidence and ability to achieve what you want.
● Confidence goes closely together with persistence; making sure it is positive needs working at.

Progress may sometimes be made only in steps. Just like the baker in the story above, there may not be a magic formula or something instantly applied that bestows instant change and thus instant confidence. But there may well be a series of steps, each of which takes you forward a little, and in so doing, makes whatever you are contemplating more able to be done, done well and without agonies of doubt.

Of course, for most of us there are some things that are beyond us, and perhaps always will be; I remain utterly without confidence that I will ever juggle with flaming torches. But there are many things that are within our capabilities to do and do well, but for which we need confidence. A good level of confidence is usually the result of consideration and action. It can make things possible, it can make things easier, and it can lift you from just coping into achieving excellence.

The process starts, as we have seen, with consideration. That consideration, and the results of it, become a habit which at best can boost confidence, in turn enhance performance, and, quite possibly, transform your life.

Surviving in tough times

Here's a safe prediction: the future looks like being uncertain. This is hardly a confidence-boosting thought, but we all know that recent times have been difficult – the banks, the economy, the Euro and more. The result is recession and low growth, and firm predictions that such a state will take some years to change. Clearly waiting for things to 'get back to normal' is simply not an option.

Whatever the business sector within which you work, all this makes things likely to be more difficult than they would be in other circumstances. This last short section offers ten key points that may help maintain the possibility of your being confident in what you do, despite difficult times, despite there being more to worry about. When there is less time to check things out, those who might help are extra busy and generally more may be expected of you, and less patience forthcoming about any shortfalls to your performance. The key issues are:

1 Recognize natural negatives

It is natural to find that you seem to be surrounded by factors that sap your confidence (including your own negative self-talk) and in an organization tackling tough times such influences can be more evident. Don't resent it, don't be submerged by it – see it as something which you can deal with.

2 A level of confidence *can* be improved

It is easy to feel that your level of confidence is fixed, just part of who you are, and this feeling is compounded by the extra pressure of tough times (as in the first point). This is not so. Believe it and, step by step, you can make improvements.

3 The 'balance' concept

To make progress more manageable, use the analogy mentioned in the text of the balance (plus and minus points on the scales). This makes it clear that there is no magic formula and that progress is easier on a step-by-step basis, one that you can monitor and from which you can draw comfort.

4 You need to work at it

This is a base principle of this book's whole message. But it is easy to be distracted when things are difficult and hectic all around you. As the old saying has it – it's difficult to see the writing on the wall when your back's to it. Be realistic, you will make no progress unless you work at it – so make sure you do so. Even small steps taken successfully can encourage you to do more.

5 Make sure of how

No amount of confidence can make you able to do things you simply do not understand how to go about. Again, hectic conditions may pressurize you into running before you can walk. Resist it: make sure you do the necessary preparation and are suitably informed before you proceed. Doing so, by definition, imbues confidence.

6 Focus on problems and solutions

Do not just have fears, analyse the situation. List what actual problems create the fear and seek specific solutions that will help you. Take comfort when this works (it does!) and make it a habit.

7 Organize people to help

Take steps to make sure you get help, advice and encouragement from others: your colleagues, your manager, a mentor, whoever. This may take more effort in an organization beset with problems, but cannot be omitted; it's a vital element.

8 Positively motivate yourself

With tough times making everything more difficult, do not neglect to motivate yourself. This may range from simply taking note of an (even small) problem solved, to giving yourself a tangible reward for some achievement (I recommend cake after succeeding in the presentation we featured!).

9 Let positive experience assist

Learn from experience. Sometimes you may feel you are making little progress (especially in tough times), but always note what goes well. It can provide simple motivation, but it can also be a proven method, so that you say to yourself that if something works well, then a similar method can be applied elsewhere.

10 Think positive, believe

There is not a great deal to be said here. You must see the glass as half full even in difficult times. Let me end by repeating a saying quoted in the introduction: *If you think you can, you can; and if you think you can't, you're right.* Or, perhaps equally apposite, it is time to quote Emile Coue: *Every day, in every way, I am getting better and better.*

Despite all the difficulties, you *can* ensure your confidence is at a reasonable level. You can tackle all you must do with a reasonable chance of success. It was said early on that there is no magic formula. Those who seem most confident doubtless work at it, and while neither you nor I may ever be confident of juggling with flaming torches, there is no reason why we should not be confident of achieving what needs to be done ... provided we work at it. This is not a book that should end by wishing readers good luck. I have surely made clear luck is not the magic formula here – but I wish you well.

Postscript: at the beginning of this book, I expressed confidence that I would reach this point successfully; and here we are. Confidence was not the only factor making this possible, of course, but it surely helped. Now, what next?

> ***If you want to do something, you find a way. If you don't want to do anything, you find an excuse.***
>
> Traditional proverb

Answers to questions

Sunday 1 b, 2 c, 3 a, 4 c, 5 b, 6 b, 7 d, 8 d

Monday 1 b, 2 c, 3 b, 4 c, 5 a, 6 c, 7 d, 8 a

Tuesday 1c, 2 b, 3 b, 4 c, 5 a, 6 b, 7 c, 8 a

Wednesday 1c, 2 b, 3 b, 4 d, 5 b, 6 c, 7 c, 8 c

Thursday 1c, 2 d, 3 b, 4 b, 5 b, 6 c, 7 b, 8 d

Friday 1 a, 2 d, 3 c, 4 b, 5 c, 6 a, 7 c, 8 b, 9 c, 10b

Saturday 1 a, 2 c, 3 b, 4 b, 5 c, 6 b, 7 a, 8 b

ALSO AVAILABLE IN THE 'IN A WEEK' SERIES

BODY LANGUAGE FOR MANAGEMENT • BOOKKEEPING AND ACCOUNTING • CUSTOMER CARE • DEALING WITH DIFFICULT PEOPLE • EMOTIONAL INTELLIGENCE • FINANCE FOR NON-FINANCIAL MANAGERS • INTRODUCING MANAGEMENT • MANAGING YOUR BOSS • MARKET RESEARCH • NEURO-LINGUISTIC PROGRAMMING • OUTSTANDING CREATIVITY • PLANNING YOUR CAREER • SPEED READING • SUCCEEDING AT INTERVIEWS • SUCCESSFUL APPRAISALS • SUCCESSFUL ASSERTIVENESS • SUCCESSFUL BUSINESS PLANS • SUCCESSFUL CHANGE MANAGEMENT • SUCCESSFUL COACHING • SUCCESSFUL COPYWRITING • SUCCESSFUL CVS • SUCCESSFUL INTERVIEWING

For information about other titles in the series, please visit www.inaweek.co.uk

ALSO AVAILABLE IN THE 'IN A WEEK' SERIES

SUCCESSFUL JOB APPLICATIONS • SUCCESSFUL JOB HUNTING • SUCCESSFUL KEY ACCOUNT MANAGEMENT • SUCCESSFUL LEADERSHIP • SUCCESSFUL MARKETING • SUCCESSFUL MARKETING PLANS • SUCCESSFUL MEETINGS • SUCCESSFUL MEMORY TECHNIQUES • SUCCESSFUL MENTORING • SUCCESSFUL NEGOTIATING • SUCCESSFUL NETWORKING • SUCCESSFUL PEOPLE SKILLS • SUCCESSFUL PRESENTING • SUCCESSFUL PROJECT MANAGEMENT • SUCCESSFUL PSYCHOMETRIC TESTING • SUCCESSFUL PUBLIC RELATIONS • SUCCESSFUL RECRUITMENT • SUCCESSFUL SELLING • SUCCESSFUL STRATEGY • SUCCESSFUL TIME MANAGEMENT • TACKLING INTERVIEW QUESTIONS

For information about other titles in the series, please visit www.inaweek.co.uk